GLOUCESTERSHIRE
BETWEEN THE WARS
A Memoir

GLOUCESTERSHIRE
BETWEEN THE WARS
A Memoir

ARTHUR STANLEY BULLOCK

The
HISTORY
Press

The author, Author Stanley Bullock (A.S.B.), photographed in 1926.

First published 2009

The History Press
The Mill, Brimscombe Port
Stroud, Gloucestershire, GL5 2QG
www.thehistorypress.co.uk

British Library Cataloguing in Publication Data.
A catalogue record for this book is available from the British Library.

ISBN 978 0 7524 4793 3

Typesetting and origination by The History Press
Printed in Great Britain

Contents

A.S. Bullock in 1987.

Editor's Preface

By A.S. Bullock's granddaughter, Rachel Beckett

My grandfather, Arthur Stanley Bullock (A.S.B.), was possibly the most inspirational person I have ever known: tireless in his infectious enthusiasm for life, formidable in his depth of knowledge and understanding, blessed with a considerable and lively intellect (even in old age) and a most generous and loving character in his conduct towards those who knew him. Naturally, I write with some degree of granddaughterly bias, and he had his share of faults, including stubbornness and a tendency to be overbearing, but I probably speak for my three siblings as well as my mother (A.S.B.'s only child) when I say that our overriding memory of him is one of delight – in his gleeful sense of humour, his endless ability to rejoice in life's marvels and, most of all, his talent for reflecting on his experiences, extracting their meaning and telling the most wonderful true stories about them.

Like the youth in his favourite poem, Gray's *Elegy Written in a Country Churchyard*, A.S.B. was obscure by accident of birth and fortune, yet had much to contribute to life, which he did.

His talent for storytelling is very evident in this fascinating memoir, beginning with a rural Edwardian childhood in the Forest of Dean, and encompassing his extraordinary experiences in the trenches of the First World War. His account continues with the privations endured as an apprentice in Birmingham and as a job seeker in South Wales during the economic difficulties of the 1920s, and later experiences working for R.A. Lister & Co. and running his own engineering works during the Second World War.

As his epitaph, my mother chose the words 'He loved truth, beauty and justice'. This might have seemed pretentious, were it not for the fact that it is true. He devoted much of his retirement to the values and ideals he continued to believe in, and often quoted the motto of Ella Wheeler Wilcox: that the one most important art in the whole world is 'just the art of being kind'.

Foreword

By A.S. Bullock's daughter, Nancy Lewis

The total eclipse of the sun on 11 August 1999 would have been my father A.S. Bullock's 100th birthday. This is appropriate because of the many coincidences and unusual events in his life. Although he did not achieve material success commensurate with his abilities, he took an active part in society and was one of the most intelligent and perceptive men I have ever met, and his observations in this book have a relevance to present day events.

Author's Preface

All history becomes subjective; in other words,
There is properly no history; only biography.

(Emerson, Essay on History)

I have always had a suspicion that writers of autobiographies must be rather conceited fellows – except in the case of those who have played a leading part in the making of history and have something special to say. What excuses therefore can I offer to myself for writing this my own story? First and best is the view expressed by Emerson in his *Essay on History* that Man is explicable by nothing less than all his history – every little bit. Secondly, I feel that it may provide my friends and relations with some explanations of actions of mine which have puzzled them in the past; and thirdly, I hope that by committing my memoirs to paper I may have the pleasure of reliving many experiences that might not otherwise have come again to mind. Finally, if further justification is needed, I can plead that it was the opinion of no less an authority than Maxim Gorky that everyone should write his own life story.

Unfortunately, in spite of my optimistic title [this memoir was originally entitled *Before I Forget – ed.*], now that I make a general review of the past, preparatory to writing it down, I am disappointed and surprised to find how much I have already forgotten. I am afraid, therefore, that this is going to be a very sketchy affair compared with the autobiographies of certain well-known people who seem to be able to remember the smallest detail from a very early age and can even repeat verbatim a conversation which took place at some casual meeting when they were three or four years old. However, it is true that throughout my life my mind seems to have photographed and indelibly printed on my brain in vivid detail a number of scenes and incidents – sometimes accompanied by a sentence (or even a smell) – which are often of a trivial and inconsequential character; but in the main only a general impression remains in which many of the details have disappeared and the edges of some of the chief characters and features have become slightly blurred. This may arise from the fact that I have always had an inclination to paraphrase and précis, endeavouring to determine the essential factors in any particular set of circumstances and get them in their proper perspective to one another and in relation to life in general, uncluttered by a lot of secondary detail.

Having thus satisfied my conscience and apologised in advance for any bare patches that might appear, I will begin my story.

A.S. Bullock

One

Longhope

Sweet was the sound when oft at evening's close,
Up yonder hill the village murmur rose;
There as I past with careless steps and slow,
The mingling notes came softened from below;
The swain responsive as the milk-maid sung,
The sober herd that lowed to meet their young;
The noisy geese that gabbled o'er the pool,
The playful children just let loose from school

(Oliver Goldsmith, *The Deserted Village*)

I have been informed that I was born at 8 a.m. on Friday 11 August 1899 in what is reputed to be the oldest dwelling house in the village of Longhope, Gloucestershire. The house at the time was known as Trombone Cottage, having been so named in a rush of musical fervour and questionable taste by my father, George Bullock, who was a devoted member of the Mitcheldean Prize Brass Band – of which more anon. My mother often complained that my birthday was one of the hottest days she could remember.

I was the last of seven children – Alice Margaret was the first (born 1 June 1887), then George Wallace (4 December 1888), Florence Mabel (21 February 1890), Lucy Mildred (8 October 1891), Ruth Jane (7 January 1894), Jack, and finally me. All grew up to adulthood except Jack, who only survived for about twenty-four hours.

There was a gap of over five years between my sister Ruth and me – a fact which influenced my life quite considerably, as I had all the advantages of being a member of a fairly large family, while living in many ways the life of an only child. Also, being the baby of the family and having been endowed with a very fair complexion, frizzy golden hair and blue eyes, I am prepared to accept the allegation which has been made that I was slightly spoilt by my mother and my much older brother and sisters, and became a little precocious, though I cannot accept responsibility for that. The rest of the family lived their lives several years ahead of me and had memories in common which I could not share. For instance, they could remember life at Trombone Cottage, whereas the only thing I can remember about the place are two slots nailed to the bottom of each door foot in which a board was inserted to prevent babies getting out into the garden.

Arthur's birthplace, Trombone Cottage. Its name betrays that his father was a brass-band enthusiast with a sense of humour!

The first house I can really remember was Hill View, Nupend Lane. When the family moved there I do not know, but it was my home for longer than any other house in Longhope. It still stands, and although I have not been inside it for over fifty years[1] I still regard it with affection. Looking back, I know that it and its situation — particularly its situation — had a profound effect on how I was going to look at the world. I think, therefore, that I should describe the house and its location in some detail.

I could hardly have chosen a better village to be born in than Longhope. The parish occupies the most easterly valley in the group of hills which lie between the Severn and the Wye. The name means long valley. It is about four miles long, running roughly north to south, and it is separated from the Severn valley by a range of hills consisting of May Hill (937ft), Huntley Hill, Blaisdon Hill and Notwood Hill. The village lies at the bottom in the centre, and the western side is the eastern flank of the Forest of Dean. The houses were sufficiently concentrated to give a sense of community and sufficiently scattered to give the citizens a sense of individuality. The Great Western Railway gave a frequent and quick service to Gloucester, ten miles away, but for shopping it was really not necessary to go outside the village as there were two good general stores with three small shops, two bakers, a post office, coal merchant, blacksmith and four public houses. During my childhood Mrs Wright opened another general shop and news agency, and Mr C. Powell built a village hall which he called Latchen Room. There was a cricket team, football team, tennis club and a choral society. Occasional concerts, socials and dances were held, and other cultural and sporting facilities were available from time to time. In addition to the church school, there was a council school next to Zion Baptist Chapel at the top of Hopes Hill.

The chief employer was the firm of James Constance and Sons, who ran saw mills and a turnery. This provided a perfect example of indigenous industry: the surrounding hills were crowned with woods of mixed timber, which were owned by the King. These were cut in rotation to a yearly timetable to feed the saw mills with birch, ash, etc. for the stick trade, with the larger timber such as oak, beech etc. being felled at maturity. If anything occurred to upset this timetable (as it did some years later), the birch and ash saplings in the wood due for cutting in a given year would grow too large for the stick trade and throw the whole rotation out of gear, so much so that

Longhope from Latchen Hill in the early years of the twentieth century.

it would take years to re-establish the rotation. I should explain that the stick trade consisted of pike handles, broom sticks, scythe handles, spade trees, rake handles, axe helves etc., where in order to get a first-class job it was desirable that the grain should run through from end to end. In this field Constance and Sons were supreme in this country, and my father was once photographed by the *Illustrated London News*, in which he appeared making a wooden rake.

Of course there were many occupations – building, hurdle-making, wheel-wrighting, manufacture of farm waggons and traps and, of course, farming. This was generally mixed farming, with each farmer having horses, cows, sheep, pigs, poultry and orchards, with a little arable land, pasture and hay fields. Many people grew apples and pears and made cider and perry, but the great fruit crop was plums. Longhope and the surrounding parishes grew thousands of tons of a plum which had been developed locally and which took its name from the adjacent parish of Blaisdon. Most of these plums went from Longhope by special goods train to the industrial towns of the north. A nearby parish of Dymock gave its name to another plum and the parish of Blakeney also gave its name to Blakeney Red Pears, from which the perry was made, and the trees of which sometimes reached a height of over 100ft. Practically all the villagers kept a pig and fowls and had a garden or orchard in which they grew vegetables and fruit.

In relation to this village Hill View occupied an isolated position, buried among fruit trees some 400ft up on the western side of the valley. It faced east, and from the front windows one could see the range of hills previously mentioned, the crest line of which for several years formed the horizon which was the boundary of my world. Behind the house the hill rose to a height of about 700ft and was crowned by a wood of mixed oak, ash, birch, holly etc. To get to the house from the valley one took the Mitcheldean Road to the top of Latchen rise, turned right up Nupend Lane, turned left through a farm gate at the top of the lane, crossed an orchard by a cart track and

Longhope from a postcard sent to Arthur by his sister Ruth in 1922. The photograph may have been taken earlier.

so arrived at our orchard, which surrounded the house and garden. A footpath went up past the house, bore south through 'The Thicket', crossed two meadows which, for some reason I have never been able to discover, were called Little Andla and Big Andla, down a hill and over a stile to rejoin the Mitcheldean Road near the house and builder's yard belonging to our landlord, Mr F. Field, commonly known as Feyther Field. He was a churchwarden, and a real character.

Hill View was a low-built cottage of red sandstone, daub and wattle, covered with stucco and pink-washed, with a red roman-tiled roof. A beamed living-room/kitchen was separated by a red, tiled passage from the 'parlour'. The staircase went up from this passage to a large landing, converted into a bedroom by use of a screen, with a bedroom on either side. Both the landing and the bedrooms were built into the roof with dormer windows. All were whitewashed. A roman-tiled lean-to on the north and west sides formed a back kitchen and a fuel store and lock-up shed, over which was a loft. Water was obtained by winch and bucket from a well in the garden, and the only sanitation was an earth closet.

The heart of the establishment and centre of nearly all our activities was the living room, which was always referred to as the kitchen. This fairly large but warm and cosy room had one deep-silled window overlooking the valley, with another opposite looking into the lean-to back kitchen. A large built-in dresser was opposite the fireplace, which contained a small range for cooking. To the left of the fireplace was a large baking oven built into the wall. A mirror over the mantelshelf reflected a muzzle loading gun hanging in leather straps from a beam. Owing to the extreme unevenness of the walls the floral wallpaper was a bit wrinkled in places. On one wall was a very old rectangular clock which gained about thirty minutes a day, and another wall was usually occupied by one or two sides of bacon hung by rope loops passing through a hole and round a stout hazel crosspiece. A large deal kitchen table stood in the centre

Longhope from Latchen Hill, here seen in winter, from a family postcard sent in 1922.

Longhope Church, school and rectory. The school, which Arthur and his siblings attended, remained in use throughout the twentieth century.

and the rest of the furniture consisted of a very old writing desk, half a dozen wooden kitchen chairs, a low wooden armchair, a rocking chair and a homemade settee. The floor was covered with coconut matting, and a homemade rag mat was the hearth rug. Lighting was by a brass oil lamp fitted with a white conical shade, which threw a pool of light onto the table but left the rest of the room in a warm gloom.

The parlour, which was only used on Sundays and special occasions, was very 'posh'. Linoleum covered the floor. Two armchairs, one of basket work, stood on either side of a high-barred grate with two little hobs. A single-ended mahogany sofa upholstered in horsehair and American leather – easily the hardest sofa I have ever sat on – stood against the opposite wall under two large framed religious texts set among a mixture of crosses, birds, flowers and angels. I regret that I cannot remember the wording of the texts, but I feel they must have had a good influence on all of us. The parlour also boasted a mahogany drop-leaf table and a mahogany chiffonier, while built against the chimney breast was a cupboard which held games, china, glasses, musical instruments – a concertina, a flute and a flageolet – together with some books, magazines and toys. A mirror over the fireplace and three or four occasional chairs of unusual design with leather loose cushion seats completed the furnishing. Of course in both the living room and the parlour there were plenty of framed photographs and vases standing on crocheted mats, and pots with indoor plants in the windows.

The furnishing of the bedrooms was minimal. The pale deal floors were bare except for a few mats. All the bedsteads were iron with straw palliasses and feather beds on top, but my parents' bed was distinguished by brass knobs on the four corners. Apart from the beds the furniture was of the scantest – a homemade dressing table in my sisters' room (disguised by muslin hangings), with a small swing mirror on top; a cupboard in my brother's room with a similar swing mirror, and a mahogany chest of drawers in my parents' room with a swing mirror. Each room had a wooden chair and a painted washstand with basin and jug. Clothes were mainly kept in tin chests under the beds, together with the inevitable chamber pot.

My parents occupied the south room over the parlour, which curiously had a door covered in green baize secured with brass-headed tacks. My brother slept on the converted landing, and my sisters had the north end room. I, too, slept in this room in a separate bed until I reached the age of 'indiscretion' (except on those occasions when they were all at home together and I was crowded out). I then had to sleep with my brother. When I grew up, and he had left home, his room became mine.

So much for the first scene, now for the actors: firstly, my mother. Her maiden name was Sarah Margaret Wallace, and she belonged to a group of families, Wallaces, Greers, McHughs and Littles, who had emigrated to Northern Ireland from Ayrshire during the Plantation of Ulster. I could never seem to nail down details of her early childhood, except that her father was a tailor who died when she was very young and that her mother, who played the organ at the local church, died at the early age of twenty-seven, leaving her an orphan to be brought up by her cousin Ruth, who had married a yeoman of substance, John Robert Greer. Their farm was in the hamlet of Hamiltons Bawn near Armagh. Because of an accident to her ankle her schooling had apparently been curtailed, but I do not think from the way she expressed herself in reading, writing and speech that anyone could have told that she had not had at least an average education. Perhaps the fact that she was extraordinarily intelligent and determined had something to do with it. She had plenty of relations in Ulster, America, Australia and New Zealand. All were Orangemen and Presbyterians, and it is not surprising that in religion she was a somewhat narrow-minded puritan with absolutely no use for anything connected with Roman Catholicism. Curiously, although of Scottish descent, she was fanatically Irish, and woe betide anyone who said a word against Ireland or the Irish. Although she spent nearly the whole of her

Hill View, Longhope, painted by Arthur when he was fourteen years old.

life in England and brought up a large family there I don't believe she was ever really at home in England. She was very small but had the heart of a lion, and if there was something she particularly wanted to do she would hear of no obstacles. Although it is comforting to be with someone who is so confident as to scoff at danger, I must say that sometimes she carried it to the point of being ludicrous. I remember one night when I was about eight years old she and I were making our way home to the lonely and empty cottage on a pitch black night when, as we were going up through the trees in the orchard, a light shone out in the fowls' yard at the side of the house. We were both surprised and I was terrified. She knew I was, and I think she was too, but putting on a bold front and saying to comfort me, 'Don't worry, I'll soon deal with that', she was off, and I was left shivering with fright, waiting for a shriek and wondering what I would do if she were murdered. However, she came back after a few minutes to report that there was nobody there. So we proceeded home, but I was not convinced and felt very unhappy until my father's homecoming brought relief.

My mother had black hair and the most beautiful eyes – grey with tawny flecks in them – and a fresh complexion. I believe she was very attractive when young, and this is confirmed by an early photograph. She was proud, and deeply religious with a strong sense of right and wrong, duty and loyalty. Her mind was lively and, although normally over-optimistic and romantic, she could become very depressed and melancholy. Although very affectionate, she could be over-severe. She could also be very perverse and pig-headed. As readers will have gathered from the foregoing, she had many Irish characteristics, but oddly she had not got a very strong sense of humour. I feel this was a great pity as I think it would have helped her to adjust herself to

Above: Arthur's mother, Sarah Bullock, with (from left to right) Floss, Lucy and Wallace.

Left: Arthur's mother, Sarah, in her youth.

the somewhat hard and unsatisfactory life she had to lead. She was skilled in all the domestic arts; she was a splendid mother and a wonderful cook. What with sewing, knitting, darning, mending, baking, cooking, housework and looking after poultry, she had practically no relaxation. During the time I knew her she never seemed to be quite well; in particular, she suffered from indigestion, and things were not helped by the fact that to counteract her complaints she starved herself and was constantly dosing herself with patent medicines.

My father was a totally different type. Short, stocky with red-gold hair, blue eyes and a very fair complexion, he looked a typical Saxon. He was strong and healthy, somewhat 'earthy', and liked good food, strong drink and good company – in short, he liked having a good time. If I was asked if he preferred play to work I couldn't say; all I know is that he was very good at both. He was one of those lucky people who seem to know instinctively the best way of doing whatever they want to do. He was born on 3 March about 1863, and for a while attended the Baptist Chapel School, or Zion School as it was called, but he could not have been there very long as he told me he was behind a plough at the age of nine. This would have been possible, as until the twentieth century ploughing in Longhope was still done with oxen. A child of nine could not have handled cart horses. He became a general farm worker and obtained a position at Newlands in the Forest of Dean, and it was possibly here that he met my

Lucy Bullock, the sister to whom Arthur was closest. Seen here in youth, she later married twice, her second husband being a member of the prosperous Wills family of Bristol.

mother, who was a cook at a gentleman's house in Goodrich. About the time of his marriage he took employment at Longhope Saw Mills, owned by James Constance, where he remained for over sixty years, being made redundant in his late eighties (due to contraction of business) without a word of thanks or any token of so many years of loyal service, mostly as a key worker, since he had invented a trapping device for bending scythe handles, which he operated.

Father was a contemporary of Lloyd George, of whom he was an admirer, and I often thought of him as the village Lloyd George. He fitted exactly the reference to a 'Village Hampden' mentioned in Gray's famous *Elegy in a Country Churchyard*. I never knew his parents, and nobody seems to know anything about them – they were not mentioned by him or his two sisters – but I heard a rumour that his mother ran away to Birmingham with another man, leaving her husband, a farm labourer, with three small children to bring up. It is possible her name was Critchley, as an old woman named Critchley and known as Granny Scratch was supposed to be related in some way, and there is a walnut

Longhope saw mills.

E.J. Hall and Son, Longhope.

box in the family with the initials SMC on it, which I believe belonged to my father's mother. My sister Lucy was told that Grandfather Bullock died by falling off a hayrick following a heart attack. I do not know where they lived.

Similarly I am not certain how my mother and father met, and I have some difficulty in imagining the courtship in view of the difference in their characters and upbringing. Unfortunately, apart from good intelligence, the thing in which each

Arthur's father, George Bullock, aged about sixty-seven, *c.* 1930. A true countryman, he was also renowned for his wit and religious scepticism. Once, on being told of the vicar's Sunday invocation, 'O Lord, give Longhope a mighty shaking!', George allegedly commented, 'That was a damn silly thing for him to say with all the plums ripe on the trees!'

Longhope Church School pupils in 1909. Arthur is near the left end of the middle row, just behind and to the left of the girl in the pale gymslip. (This is not the first photo alluded to in the text.)

most resembled the other was not a characteristic which made for unity – I refer to a quick, fiery temper allied to extreme stubbornness.

As for my brother and sisters, they seemed to emerge on my consciousness as if out of a mist. I simply do not remember Alice, Wallace or Floss as children. Lucy and Ruth were at school when I first attended, but Lucy left almost immediately afterwards and Ruth a couple of years later while I was still in the infants' class. In the case of Alice and Floss, because they had to go into domestic service at a very early age, they had left home before I had really got to know them. Poor Alice, at eleven years old, became a servant to a schoolmaster living in a small house in Worcester Street, Gloucester, although she was a girl of great intelligence. My first memories of Alice are of a good-looking, superior young lady, slim in build with light brown hair and grey eyes. In contrast, Floss was shorter and inclined to plumpness with dark brown eyes and almost black hair; altogether a warm-looking person. Wallace was well built, of medium height, fresh complexion, pale blue eyes and light brown hair. Girls thought him handsome. Before he went off to south Wales he tried to enlist in some crack regiment as a regular soldier, but he was not tall enough.

Until Lucy, too, entered domestic service at the age of thirteen, she seems to have been given the unenviable task of seeing that her baby brother arrived at school and elsewhere on time and in a presentable condition – hair combed, face washed, boots cleaned and clothes properly adjusted, but whether this task was self-imposed or under instructions I do not know. Perhaps she even enjoyed doing it. Of course, I had more to do with Ruth than the rest as she was only five years older. She had coal-black hair, a pale skin and hazel eyes. I'm afraid she was a bit of a tomboy; also, rather scatter-brained and dreamy, but she was musical and loved reading.

You will be hearing more about each as my story develops, but I thought I had better introduce them. They were all intelligent, all musical and all very interesting, as they differed widely with strong individualities.

The first photograph in the book[2] shows me in petticoats at the age of two. From the wheelbarrow and hand fork my interest in gardening appears to have started early. The little dog, Gyp, lived for many years after the photograph was taken. The second photo shows me in petticoats at the front of a group of children at the Longhope Church School, which confirms the fact that I attended school (though not regularly) before I was three years old. I wonder if this is a record? Lucy or Ruth must have taken me. What astonishes me is not so much that I was there but how I got there. The shortest possible distance from Hill View to the school was three quarters of a mile across fields, and it is certain that I must have walked both ways because there was no alternative. Alas for the petticoats. Looking at them now I find them very charming but by the time I commenced school regularly at the age of three they had been replaced by boys' clothing. My mother told me that the day she tried on my knickerbockers for fit (she had made them herself) I refused to take them off and stamped on the petticoats. I have a vague memory of the actual incident, which took place in the entrance to the parlour at Hill View. Probably that is my earliest memory, but it was about this time that by standing on tiptoe my eyes came above the level of the kitchen table top and a wonderful new world was revealed, in somewhat the same way as the Pacific Ocean was revealed to 'stout Cortez on a peak in Darien'!

I think I must have been kept at home for the first winter as I distinctly remember that one day, when the others were at school, I first tried my hand at painting. While Mother was baking I discovered in one of the cupboards a nice polished wooden box of watercolours. We had a meat safe fixed to the wall of the back kitchen, the wood of which was not painted or varnished. I thought this deficiency should be rectified and finally achieved a kind of spectrum of colour down one side of the door frame. Delighted at my achievement I called my mother's attention to it. She agreed that she had a most artistic son but not until several years later was I allowed to see or use those paints again. My work of art was still there fifteen years later when I said goodbye to Hill View.

When I think of the way children of today are coddled and transported from home to school on buses etc. I can hardly believe that for some eight years from three to eleven I walked across fields for nearly a mile in all winds and weathers, and for the last six of those years I was never once absent or late. But of course there were children who lived much farther away than I did. A crippled boy called Grosvenoe, who was also an epileptic for good measure, lived at the Parish Mill on the Mitcheldean road at least two miles from the school, and he won a gold medal for regular attendance and punctuality for several years. A whole contingent of children came from May Hill. They were called 'the gorse bush jumpers'. I can see them now, like one of the tribes of Israel over Hard Head (or 'Ard Yud as it was commonly pronounced) – the Reads, Warners, Pithouses and Pensoms, both sexes and all ages and sizes, running about and shouting, over the brook, through the churchyard and up the school lane, joining with the Carters, Hooks, Hawkins and Simmonds from the Upper End of the village and the Bowketts, Hendys, Carpenters, Browns and Bullocks plus a few others from the village itself. Two things intrigued me about the children from May Hill – their calf development, characteristic of hill men, and the extraordinary glow on their faces. It was as though they had been French polished! I have never seen anything like it elsewhere.

I want to emphasise that I have no complaints about my childhood. I would not have changed it for that of anyone else. Had my parents been better educated, richer, or in a higher social station they might have been able to make my entry into the big world a little easier, but I am sure they did their best for me and the rest of the family according to their means and their lights. I have never had much use for alibis or excuses for normal healthy persons, though I agree with Shakespeare that 'there is a Destiny that shapes our ends, rough hew them how we will'. From our very earliest days it was made clear to all of us children that we were responsible for our own actions. It was also made clear to us by both Mother and Father, who were fierce individualists, that as people we were inferior to nobody, not even the King, and while we were to behave with courtesy to everyone, we were to be subservient to no one. Long before I was born Longhope had ceased to have a squire as such, but there was a lady of the manor, to whom my sister Alice innocently admitted in the presence of my father that she had curtsied. She was strictly forbidden to ever again curtsey to anyone and I am sure she never did.

In explanation of our attitudes to life perhaps I ought to add that our parents impressed on us that whatever we undertook it was our duty to endeavour to do it better than anyone else. This was summed up in a ditty our mother repeatedly sang to us:

If I were a tinker no tinker beside
Would mend an old kettle like me,
Let who will be second,
The first I'm determined to be.

I can't answer for my brother and sisters as to how far they carried this into their lives. I can only say that at school, at work and at play I have always played to win, but if defeated I have tried to accept it with good grace. As regards ditties to lend point to some lesson, Mother seemed to have an endless supply, and even up to the end of her life she could trot out a new one to surprise me. How, in her short education, she could have accumulated such a stock I shall never know. Of all the family my most continuous relationship was with my mother. Contact with my father and Wallace was daily but intermittent as they were at work, and of course I only saw Alice and Floss when they were on holiday or between jobs. That was true of Lucy and Ruth, too, when they left for service, but until then we were fairly close, especially when I was a small boy at Longhope School.

A typical day at Hill View would start just before 7 a.m. with the noise of my parents going downstairs. Then my father would rouse Wallace in the middle room and I would hear them leave the house just before or about the same time that the hooter at the saw mills sounded (as a family we were not very good in the morning). I would hear the noise of pots and pans as Mother prepared our breakfast in the living room below. Then

Longhope against the backdrop of May Hill, with its then sparse crown of trees (the photograph is from a postcard sent to Arthur by his eldest sister, Alice, in 1927). George Bullock, Arthur's father, was the member of the Parish Council responsible for the trees. He must have done a good job, as the hilltop is now thick with them!

the smell of frying bacon mixed perhaps with woodsmoke would permeate the house and – if it was early summer – mingle with the scent of honeysuckle, musk and other flowers and the light scent of fruit blossom drifting in through the window, which was permanently open because the honeysuckle had grown round the casement. I would lie and enjoy this while looking up at the whitewashed open ceiling, watching the endless and apparently aimless flying round and round of a small cloud of houseflies, wondering if there was any plan to their gyrations and how they decided it was time to change direction. Chattering from the other bed would indicate that Lucy and Ruth were awake. Presently Mother would call from below and Lucy would get up and dress, but it would take more than one call to get Ruth and myself downstairs as we were both 'slugabeds'. The saw mill's hooter would signal the breakfast break at 8 a.m. and shortly afterwards Dad and Wallace would return. By then Mother would have had her breakfast and be ready to read 'Proceedings in Parliament' to my Father from the *Morning Leader* while he had his breakfast. We all had to be very quiet while this almost religious ceremony took place. Our breakfast finished, we kids prepared for school. Lucy took me out into the back kitchen, washed my hands and scrubbed my face with red carbolic soap and cold water from the well, contained in a red glazed earthenware bowl placed upon a homemade bench. She put on my celluloid Eton collar, as I slept in my shirt, tied my bow and brushed my hair. Then, when she had washed, brushed her own auburn curls and generally tidied herself up we set off for school.

Lucy had the same build as Alice but different colouring. Her eyes were brown and she had the most lovely shining thick auburn hair, full of waves and curls that it would be possible to see. In later life as a servant her beautiful hair was often commented on by employers, as it no doubt looked very attractive piled up under a lace cap. The 8.30 hooter at the mill would by now have signalled the end of breakfast break and theoretically Dad and Wallace should have returned to work, but it would surprise me if they ever got back anywhere near 8.30. However, nobody seemed to mind.

With us all out of the house Mother would clear away the breakfast and wash up in an old tin bowl with hot water from a big iron kettle which was always boiling on the hob, then feed the pig with swill and household scraps and the fowls with maize, or Indian corn as we called it, and collect the eggs. The dog and cat having been attended to, the house cleaned and the beds made, she would prepare dinner for Dad and Wallace. We kids often took sandwiches to school as it was rather a long way to get home and back in the time allowed. Dinner finished, Mother would probably settle down to sewing, knitting or darning. Then about 4.30 we would be home for tea, which would consist of homemade bread, butter, homemade jam and a wide variety of homemade cakes. Ruth and I might go out to play but Lucy would have some job to do either for Mother or sewing or knitting for herself.

Shortly after 6 o'clock Dad and Wallace would arrive with the evening paper, *The Gloucester Citizen*. There was always a plate of soft cheese for Dad which had been toasted in the oven, and when I was very small, when I happened to be in, Dad would sometimes allow me to sit on his corduroyed knee and receive titbits of bread and the said cheese. After giving the pig his evening meal Dad would probably spend some time in the garden or making something like hen coops or chicken runs, then he would come in for a wash and brush up and retire to the Yew Tree public house for a game of cards or dominoes and a pint (or more) of beer. Wallace, meantime, would smarten himself up very much and go off to join his cronies in the village, or take his bicycle and set off to see his latest girlfriend of whom there seemed to be legions.

Mother would probably resume the sewing, knitting or darning until supper time. At dusk the brass paraffin lamp would be transferred to the centre of the kitchen table (by then covered with a maroon or green baize cloth). When lit, this gave a good circle of light on the table but left the rest of the room pretty dim. In this circle of light would be placed any sewing, reading or games. Supper would usually consist of bread, cheese and pickles with cider or cocoa to drink, but occasionally there might be meat and cold potatoes. Sometime between 10 and 11 p.m. would see the return of Dad and Wallace, who would partake of supper and go to bed.

Of course there were lots of variations to this routine. Monday was washing day, with a corrugated scrubbing board instead of a washing machine, and this meant that ironing had to be done as and when it could during the week. Tuesdays and Fridays were baking days in the oven built into the wall. As the oven door was in the kitchen this entailed moving some furniture and spreading what was to be baked all over the kitchen. This was an awful nuisance so eventually the oven door in the living room was blocked off and an opening was made into the oven from the back kitchen. I did not mind where the oven door was but, boy, did I like baking days! Just to think of coming home from school and seeing and smelling all those goodies spread out on the table and on the floor waiting to go in the oven or cooling off makes my mouth water even now. Those lovely rich lardy cakes made with homemade lard from the pig, those big brown currant dough cakes oozing with dripping, those apple turno-vers, apple cobs, jam tarts, but most of all that bread. This was always of the cottage loaf type with crisp hard crusts, and to put butter on it was almost a sin as it tasted so delicious without it. We were, of course, lucky in that we had the ideal fuel for baking in this way, for in shaping the various tool handles at the saw mills a lot of slivers of wood were produced which we called 'chips'. These were available for nothing. They burned readily and fiercely, leaving very little ash. The technique was to fill the oven with the chips, set them alight and, when burnt out, rake out the ash, fill the oven, which was all aglow, with the things to be baked, and seal the door with wet rags. Perhaps some of the tang of the wood ash got into the bread and cakes but it was food for the Gods and I have never tasted anything to equal it since.

This reminds me of a lecture I attended a few years ago. It was one of a series on 'Industrial History' run by the Workers' Educational Association. The lecturer was a brash young graduate from Bristol University, and he was referring to the economic and social state of England just before 1914. He was commiserating with the lower classes and comparing their low standard of living with that of the lower classes in our present 'affluent society'. From his remarks one gathered that the former were half starving. I interrupted him to say that I was the oldest person present and probably the only one who had any real memory of the period. I said that just to put the record straight I felt it my duty to state that whatever else the pre-1914 lower classes lacked, it was not food, which was cheap and abundant, and any sympathy on that score was misplaced, being more applicable to the lower classes of the present so-called 'affluent' state. The fact is that we lived like fighting cocks. We grew all our own vegetables, soft fruits, apples, plums and pears. We had our own eggs, poultry, bacon and pork. Mother made a wide variety of homemade wines, as well as mushroom ketchup and pickles, and we had plenty of cider and perry. In fact a jug of cider or perry was always on the table at midday and at supper. We also produced some of our own medicines – rasp-berry vinegar for hard coughs, blackcurrant tea for colds and hot cider with rosemary and ginger for fevers. There is nothing like the last to make you sweat. It was all I had for measles, and believe me those measles went in double quick time. Two other inter-esting recipes were nettle beer as a laxative and for cleansing the blood, and inhaling the steam from ivy leaves steeped in boiling water as an antidote for influenza.

Speaking of food reminds me of my first visit to Gloucester, ten miles from home. As a treat my sister Alice took me by train to visit a friend in Hopewell Street, which is one of those miserable streets where the doors of the red brick terraced houses open direct onto the pavement of depressing Staffordshire blue bricks. We had tea in the back room, which looked out through heavy lace curtains onto a yard also paved with blue bricks. I took a poor view of the tea and the whole set-up. Walking along the street on the way home Alice said 'What's the matter? You don't seem to have enjoyed your treat.' I said, 'No, I didn't, and what a funny kitchen with no bacon hanging on the wall.' She laughingly explained that it was not usual to have bacon on the wall in town houses. But that was something new in my experience. It showed that townspeople were more dependant on shops than on themselves, and that is of course why poverty hits town dwellers harder than country folk.

Friday night was choir practice night for me. It was also band practice night for

Longhope Church choir, *c*. 1910. Arthur is third from the right in the front row.

Dad and Wallace, who were enthusiastic members of the Mitcheldean Prize Brass Band. Dad played the double bass – the biggest instrument of the lot – and Wallace played the euphonium. Dad's instrument was too big to carry to and fro over the two miles to Mitcheldean, but Wallace brought his home with him, and when he set out for practice he would go outside and blow a blast on it. This was to inform Chris Jones (or Billy Foggy as he was generally called), the band's cornetist, who lived three quarters of a mile north, that Wallace was setting out and would meet him at the top of Chesgrove Lane to walk over Breakharts Hill to Mitcheldean. Billy Foggy would answer with a blast on his cornet, which could easily be heard in the quiet night. This meant 'heard and understood'.

I know that many funny things have been said about village bands, but this band must be unique. I could never get a satisfactory answer about the 'prize' part of the name. There seemed to be a general impression that a prize had been won at some time or other but nobody seemed to know when or where. To me the thought was inconceivable. Anyway, by fair means or foul, they had secured an annual engagement at Birdlip on the Cotswold escarpment. I believe they provided the 'music' for some chapel celebrations. Probably it was an anniversary. At home we called it 'Birdlip Sunday', and it was a red-letter day in the calendar, for when they had fulfilled their engagement the horse brake which conveyed them always brought them back to our place in the afternoon. Chairs and benches were provided in the orchard, with a couple of fowl houses as a back-cloth, and there they played their repertoire through until they became too exhausted or too befuddled to know what they were playing. Equipped with two water jugs from the wash-hand basin sets upstairs, my job was to

Gloucester Cathedral, which inspired Arthur's love of history and architecture, from a photograph in his treasured book, *The Story of Gloucester Cathedral* by G.H. Cook (Phoenix House, London, 1952).

Gloucester Public Library, not far from the original site of Sir Thomas Rich's School in Eastgate Street.

keep up a sort of shuttle service between the band and the cider casks. This developed into a sort of competition between me and them – me trying to keep the pint mugs full and them trying to keep them empty. As the cider, or perry, was very strong, the day usually hot, and as they had probably tried to quench their thirst on the way home from Birdlip, it does not take much imagination to realise that some progressive deterioration in the quality of the music was inevitable. A point was reached where one could only explain the noise that resulted by assuming that some members had omitted to turn over to the next piece, or had turned the pages backwards. The timing also became a little erratic, and as afternoon drew into evening fewer and fewer seemed to be playing. I must admit though that I never saw one of them trying to blow through the wrong end of the instrument. Two players in particular interested me – George Powell, the bandmaster, with a cherry-red face, and Billy Marfell, with a grey goatee beard and a white silk scarf around his throat. When George Powell could no longer conduct and Billy Marfell could not blow, then I knew that my services were no longer required. Somehow they all got back into the horse brake, and Birdlip Sunday was over.

If in reading the foregoing anyone is tempted to sneer at such a performance, let me say at once that while the standard of music may not have been perfect, the musical stamina exhibited was extraordinary. It is my belief that in similar trying circumstances the Mitcheldean Brass Band could have blown any other band into the ground and still have been producing instrumental noise of some sort. Perhaps it was for this outstanding ability that the prize previously referred to had been awarded. If further proof of their prowess is required one has only to consider the phenomenal performance at Christmas time. Commencing on Christmas Eve, breaking off late on Christmas morning and resuming on Christmas Night and Boxing Day, the band made a round of pubs, farms and the larger residences in the Mitcheldean and Longhope area, which totalled a considerable distance. At each place visited they had Christmas cheer, which included whisky, gin, brandy, rum, beer, wines, cider and perry on a scale which makes it incredible that anyone but Superman could have finished the course set in the bitterly cold weather at the time. Some of them never did. I only wish I could have been privileged to hear the Mitcheldean Prize Brass Band play when all of the players were fully sober at the same time. When the Mitcheldean Band ceased I do not know, probably it was killed off by the 1914–18 war, but I do know that the instruments were taken over by a newly formed Longhope band of which my father was the conductor for many years, and he led the band on a march through the village in celebration of the end of the Second World War. He must then have been about eighty-one. Wallace had long since left Longhope and had played for some of the best bands in South Wales.

It was worthy of note that Father and Wallace had learnt all the music they knew – and that was considerable – in a village band. Mother was very much against Wallace's membership of the band and would have fought tooth and nail to prevent me joining, but she need not have bothered as I never had any inclination to do so. My only practical connection with the band was of a menial character and involved the cleaning and polishing of Dad's instrument, for which I sometimes received the noble sum of one penny. Although fond of music, I was never fond enough to master a musical instrument. Mother paid for me to have piano lessons with Miss Ivy Wright, but I did not like being taught by a woman and just could not bring myself to concentrate on it while there were birds' nests to find or football to be played. So the only other instrumentalist in the family was Ruth, who loved the piano. I should add that Wallace also played the violin. In those days instruments were not the prohibitive price which they are today, and people of humble means had the chance to become musicians if they had the talent.

Although I liked school I always looked forward to Saturday and Sunday. I know it is not true, but I have always felt that each had an indefinable something about them that distinguished them from each other and made both different from other days of the week. Mind you, there were things about these days that I did not like very much. During the week I was expected, as soon as I was old enough, to run errands, fetch the milk before I went to school, chop wood and other odd jobs, but on Saturday mornings there were certain set jobs to be done which I hated, particularly cleaning of the knives, forks and spoons. For the benefit of those born in the stainless-steel age I had better explain that pre-stainless steel table knives became very quickly stained. Keeping them clean was quite a problem, and it was commonly done by rubbing them on a knife board surfaced with a leather strip onto which one dusted knife powder. For extra speed the blade was sometimes rubbed with a cut potato dipped in the said powder. If the weather was suitable I also had to weed the garden paths, from the gate to the front and back doors. These jobs done, I received my weekly pocket money of one penny. While I was thus engaged, my mother and sisters would be scrubbing the floors of the hall, living room and back kitchen, and sometimes the bedroom floors as well, and thoroughly sweeping and dusting the whole place. Dad and Wallace would be at work until 1 p.m.

Longhope Church, where Arthur was a member of the choir. Members of the Bullock family continued to attend the church throughout the twentieth century.

Except for a few horrid occasions, which I will refer to later, 2 o'clock on Saturday saw the 'opening of the gates of Arcady'. Summer afternoons were spent on the cricket field – the Blacksmith's meadow – and winter afternoons on the football field – sometimes watching, sometimes playing. In the cricket season we had tea at the ground and did not get home until late, but after football it was heavenly to get home to a nice warm kitchen, semi-dark before the lamp was lit, to find tea laid and the flames from the fire causing flickering lights on the glazed cups; then to consume a mountain of toast saturated in salty beef dripping or homemade lard. Some time in the afternoon or evening there would be the joy of going to Mrs Wright's shop and exchanging my one penny pocket money for some of the treasures to be found in her Aladdin's cave. In order to get the best value for money in these transactions it was necessary to apply a good deal of thought. I could not approve of the reckless abandon with which some of my friends disposed of similar amounts of cash, but I was not rigidly conservative. Rather, I would describe my approach to the problem as cautiously adventurous. It is true that I always included a farthing lucky bag, and with it sherbert and a liquorice sucking tube; but I did sometimes have aniseed balls instead of acid drops. Also, wrapped caramels at twelve for a penny made a nice change, and sometimes I even went so far as to buy a bar of chocolate, but that was usually when I had been able to wheedle a penny or two out of my wealthy sisters. On the whole, and after a great deal of experience, I should say that aniseed balls gave the best return for the money. They lasted a very long time, during which one could see the gradual changes in colour, with of course the acquired skill of efficient and even sucking necessary to make the successive layers appear evenly. But unfortunately their long-lasting qualities proved a disadvantage on those occasions when one accidentally got a half-sucked aniseed ball stuck in one's gullet and had to endure agonies until it dissolved.

Saturday evenings found everybody pretty relaxed and congenial, and even Mother might sit down for a few minutes and read the paper or a magazine. After Saturday, Sunday. A somewhat disorganised morning with a desultory breakfast, everybody a bit edgy and Dad and Wallace rather at a loss to know what to do with themselves. The rest of us, except Mother, hurried to wash and dress ourselves up in our Sunday clothes to get to morning service at church, all getting in one another's way and loudly demanding of Mother where everything was that we could not find. Mother, as usual, trying to meet everybody's demands and answer everybody's questions. After church, home to a first-class dinner prepared by Mother in our absence, after which there could be an 'explosion'. Let us assume on this particular Sunday that all the family is present but Alice. Wallace, always spoiling for an argument, asks Lucy, 'What was old Barr like this morning? Did he tell you all that rubbish about Adam and Eve and the Garden of Eden?' To which Lucy might reply, 'If you wanted to know what Mr Barr said why didn't you come to church and find out? Anyway whatever he said it would not be as much rubbish as you talk.' Wallace isn't going to let the matter rest there, so he comes back with, 'That's the worst of women; they can't argue properly. You can't get away from the fact that Darwin proved that what the Bible says is a lot of tripe. I'll lend you my Harmsworth History of the World', (which was then coming out in weekly parts), 'and then you can argue from an informed position.' By now Floss and Ruth are straining to join in, but Mother gets in first with 'Don't you bring those wicked books into this house, or I'll burn them, as I have told you before.' To this Wallace retorts, 'That's it. You can't face the truth – none of you.' This remark really gets things going and in a few minutes there is pandemonium. At last, with everybody upset, my father hits the table with his fist, glowers across at Wallace and in a voice that drowns everybody else shouts, 'That's enough.' And enough it is.

During this uproar I have been a silent observer, having no very decided views to deliver, and I now set off for Sunday school leaving the protagonists to recover their equanimity and go their various ways. I am afraid these after-dinner wrangles took place all too frequently on Sundays, and Wallace was usually the instigator. They were interesting and possibly useful in that they forced the protagonists to adjust to ideas other than their own, but they were a bit upsetting, especially for Mother, who saw some of her cherished beliefs and prejudices being very roughly treated. When I returned from Sunday school all would be calm, and Sunday tea would be taken in an atmosphere as quiet as that of the dinner was rowdy, probably because Wallace had gone out. Following an after-dinner snooze, Mother would have tidied herself up and donned her best dress, with possibly a clean white apron, and Dad would have smartened himself up a bit too. After tea I should be off to church again with my sister (it was the same distance as the school), after which, if it was a summer's evening, we might go for a walk or join Mother in a visit to the Carpenters or the Lanes. In the winter the evening would probably be spent in the parlour in front of a huge fire which made the room like an oven. Sometimes if Dad came home early from his drinks at the Yew Tree we might have a session of hymn singing. There was no accompanying instrument, but that did not matter as everybody was musical and singing in parts came naturally to us all. Alice was an excellent soprano, Wallace a good tenor and Dad a good bass. Mother had quite a sweet voice and Floss, Lucy and Ruth would sing either alto or soprano as required. In fact I don't think the Trapp Family in *The Sound of Music* would have had anything over the Bullock family at all.

My father once told the Revd George Barr that his family could 'lick the Longhope Church Choir into a cocked hat.' Perhaps an exaggeration, but we were pretty good. It amazes me how many of my contemporaries learned the hundreds of hymns they knew from the Ancient and Modern hymn book, the Alexander hymn book, Moody & Sankey, the Presbyterian hymn book, and the Bristol tune book, even allowing for the many services we attended.

Visits to the Carpenters and the Lanes were my mother's favourites, but there was a lot of visiting in families, especially in the winter, usually to play cards, the most popular games being Don, Whist or Cribbage, but at Christmas time there would be games too. There was always a good supper and plenty of cider. I liked best the evenings spent at the Halls' – the local carpenter and wheelwright – and I think Alice and Lucy must have done too, for Alice married Harry Hall and Lucy was more than fond of his brother Fred. These visits usually ended between midnight and 1 a.m. Modern child experts would condemn the keeping of small children up so late, but it did not seem to have an adverse effect except when I started school at Gloucester and had to do homework and catch the bus at 7 a.m. Then the late nights became a bit of a strain.

Modern educationists, too, would have been horrified at the way we were educated. Longhope Church School was one big room with a fire grate at one end, windows well above eye level, and when I started just some green baize curtains to divide the infants' department from the main school, later replaced by a folding wood and glass screen. There was a small lobby in which to hang coats, earth closets and a urinal for boys, all of which stank to high heaven, and no washing facilities but a tin bowl and a chunk of red carbolic soap. Canteens had not even been thought of. Winter mornings were often bitterly cold. Even when there was a roaring fire the heat could not be felt in the middle of the room, but the draught from the grate was not very good and often the fire did not really get going until about noon. Many a day I have sat for hours shivering with my feet so cold I could not feel them and my hands so cold that I could only write with difficulty, but I would be prepared to lay a large bet that, age for age, the children taught in that school on the average had a better knowledge of arithmetic, English, history, geography, the Bible, drawing, including perspective, and general knowledge than children taught by modern methods in our modern glass, centrally heated, super-hygienic palaces. They could all read and write – even the backward ones – and most of them could spell correctly. What is more, they knew the difference between right and wrong, what constituted good behaviour, and they believed that Britain was the best and the greatest country in the world – worth dying for if necessary.

The chief credit for all of this must go to Mr Hill and his wife who, with a pupil teacher, made up the staff. The mornings began with prayers, then readings by pupils from the Bible. This was followed by the whole school, including the infants, chanting the multiplication tables and division tables up to 12 x 12. The chant went 'Three times three is nine; three into nine goes three,' and so on. In this way the youngest pupils were quickly forced to learn their tables. The method may have been crude but it was effective, and no visiting inspectors ever got the wrong answers. If he asked a pupil 'What is 7 x 8?' that pupil's mouth came open and automatically said '56.' In this way even the dullest child knew his tables thoroughly. Grace was sung before and after lunch, and the day ended with a hymn.

Mr Hill was a somewhat strict master. His right arm was withered, but this did not seem to handicap him much either in writing or in using the cane, which was pretty often in use; but the cane was accepted in a sporting spirit, and various techniques were employed to minimise its effect. It was reported that a horse hair placed on the palm in line with the axis of the cane could split it, but I never saw it do so. Withdrawing the hand was a natural reaction, but this was counter-productive as it meant a double dose of caning. Thick corduroy trousers were the best protection. To illustrate the children's attitude to the cane, one day several children were caned one after the other for some misdemeanour, and when he had finished Mr Hill looked round and said, 'Well, does anyone else want the cane?' One of the older boys stood up and said 'Yes sir, I do.' 'Right,' said Mr Hill and gave him six of the best for insolence. But that boy was a hero for some time to come.

I thoroughly enjoyed school – cane and all, as that was just part of the system – but I enjoyed holidays equally. I know that schoolmasters should not have favourites, but it must be hard for them not to, which remark must act as an apology for the confession that I was a bit of a favourite with Mr Hill. Perhaps it was because I did do my best to do better than everybody else and on the whole I did tell the truth when challenged. In fact Mr Hill seemed to have got the idea that I was incapable of a lie, an opinion that not only saved my own skin on several occasions but enabled me to sometimes mitigate the punishment of my chums, for, when misbehaviour had taken place at or on the way to school, Mr Hill often asked for my version and invariably accepted it. Perhaps that was bad for my ego but it was very nice at the time.

At eleven years old I was top of the school academically, although several of the pupils were a year or two older than me. One afternoon Mr Hill called me over to his desk and showed me an advertisement in the *Gloucester Citizen*, to the effect that a County Scholarship examination would be held on such and such a date in Gloucester. He asked if I would like to sit for it, and when I hesitated he suggested I spoke to my parents and told them that he thought I would pass easily.

I should point out that things were very different then from what they are now. Most working-class people wanted their children to start earning as soon as possible and could not afford to pay for their food, clothes, train fares and sundries necessary to keep a child at school until the age of sixteen – even if by virtue of a scholarship school fees and if books were free – so some consideration was required. However, after talking it over with Mr Hill my parents agreed, and I duly sat for the exam with 130 other boys in the hall of Sir Thomas Rich's School, Gloucester. Practically all of these boys came from city schools with far better facilities than Longhope, and I had received no coaching at all. I did not know anybody and felt very nervous, but I did not find the questions particularly hard. The result was that I passed, and when I went for the oral examination I was given to understand that I had come out top in the written examination, and I was one of those privileged to choose either Sir Thomas Rich's School or the Crypt Grammar School. As at the time the Crypt was regarded as somewhat 'snooty' and academic rather than practical, and Sir Thomas Rich's practical rather than academic, I chose Sir Thomas Rich's school. Incidentally I was the first boy from Longhope to win a scholarship to a grammar school.

So my schooldays at Longhope were ended. So, too, ended a carefree halcyon period which was not to be repeated. If heaven is even half as good as life was then I shall be satisfied. But before I turn the page for the next chapter I feel I must crave indulgence while I set out on a journey of remembrance round the village, for although I lived in the village for six more years the centre of my world had changed.

As I glance round the school before saying farewell I can see again the miniature loaf of bread Mrs Hill made on my first day in the infants' class, the place where Donald Warner (aged about six) sat on the floor while being caned, calmly took off his boot and threw it at Mr Hill, the same Mr Hill pacing up and down swishing the cane after thrashing three or four boys and asking the question already mentioned 'Is there anybody else who would like a good hiding before I put the cane away?' and the astonishing response of 'Baggy' Hook with his ginger thatch, freckles, Norfolk jacket and his father's cut-off corduroy trousers standing up and saying 'I do, Sir.' Of course his voluminous trousers rendered him almost immune to the effects of caning. My sister Ruth rushing out and challenging Mr Hill in my defence after I had been punished for something, and she herself getting the cane for impudence; a line of mud-stained boys filing in about 3 o'clock in the afternoon on their return from following the hounds which had passed through the playground at about 11 a.m. and getting a swipe on each hand in consequence, resulting in Wilfred Head collapsing in a faint, which caused an awful fuss.

I pass out into the playground and think of the countless games of Gentleman's Rush, Tag, Prisoner Base, Hats on Backs, Slides, Five Stones, Hopscotch and Rounders we played there. Then I come to Coppola, a lane leading out of the yard, where among the bushes which used to cover the banks I found in a bunch of nettles my one and only Nettle Creeper's (or Jenny Whitethroat's) nest, exquisitely made mainly of black horse hair and moss with five green mottled eggs inside. From where I stand I can see that big matted hawthorn tree which had in its centre a jay's nest, the rifling of which caused so many scratches and torn clothes. I go through the gate into a field which rises steeply to one corner where there are a couple of oaks. This field was our summer playground. Football and cricket were played on the flattened bottom end, and in the hoop season a slightly risky game was played which involved one side bowling iron hoops down the bank and the other side endeavouring to catch them. It was about there that the goal-post stood, where one snowy day Stanley Radbourne and I had a set-to which resulted in the snow being stained with blood from, I am pleased to say, his nose.

And this wooden bridge under the oak trees spans Barley Brook. You will look in vain for the name in any map, and today it is partly a cart track and partly a depository for cans and old bedsteads, but when I was young only a poet could describe it adequately. A limpid stream falling over a series of small moss-grown waterfalls into pools in the red marl. It was at the bottom of a deep cleft with steep, ferny banks all hidden under hazel, aspen, holly, blackberry, yew and wild cherry trees, and in the bubbles at the foot of each waterfall it was certain one would find one or more rainbow trout asking to be tickled out onto the bank. Upstream was an ancient stone sheep wash, and in the bushes and banks were all sorts of birds, including kingfishers and dippers. Even now I shudder as I remember five or six boys climbing a yew tree to a red squirrel's nest in which were a number of newly born squirrels like limp sausages without hair. The first boy, who I believe was Harry Pithouse, dropped these one by one onto the heads of the boys beneath, of whom I was one – ugh!

The next two fields belong to Mr Palmer, and I can smell now the indescribably sweet and subtle scent of a permanent grass field just before mowing, with its legion of wildflowers – hen and chickens, cuckoo flowers, sorrel, etc. We kids knew all the best places for apples, pears, plums, blackberries, chestnuts, horse chestnuts and hazel nuts for miles around, and right in the middle of this next field stood one of the two Tom Thumb pear trees in the district. The fruit was small but very sweet. It would never pay to pick it, and so we ate it. I suppose we were technically stealing, but no such idea ever entered our heads. All boys just helped themselves to fruit wherever they found it to eat as a snack, but they did not do any wanton damage nor take valuable fruit.

Over two stiles on each side of Hengrove Lane and into Penwarden Field, where once, in the dark, coming home from choir practice I fell over a recumbent cow. The next field (also Mr Penwarden's) was filled with mixed fruit trees, and I particularly remember the trees in the corner loaded with brilliant red cider apples called tipplers. It has always been a mystery to me why coarse sour apples always seemed to be more prolific than sweet dessert ones. The footpath was close to the hedge on the top side of the field to avoid a depression, in which was a spring enclosed by huge flat stones on edge. The water was always at the same level, always crystal clear and at an almost constant temperature. It was known as Chalcroft and, like a number of these springs, it must have been very ancient. It was to this spring that we came for water when in a hot summer our own well dried up. This spot is particularly nostalgic for me because I was often met here on my way home by our tortoiseshell cat, which, hearing my whistle in the distance, would leave the hearthrug and come some 500 yards across the field and conduct me home with its tail in the air. The other memory evoked by this spot is not so pleasant. For a reason I can't explain, I had on several occasions a premonition that when I got home I should find my Mother dead, and I was so relieved when I found her busy about the place with a nice fire going and tea ready.

Over the stile I am in Dark Lane, which ran along the bottom of our back orchard and Parry's garden as an extension of Nupend Lane. I have only to turn up right through two small fields and I am home, but I stop at the gate by the pond and think of all the many times I have slammed this gate behind me. It was my entrance to the world. Sometimes coming home as a little boy alone in the dark, I approached it with my heart in my mouth, but once I passed through it and heard it bang behind me I knew I was safe. But when, also in the dark, I had to pass through it in an outward direction and I thought of all the horrid people who might be lying in wait for me in the dark lane, it was then that I really did slam the gate with a bang – a bang of defiance to let the lurkers know that I did not care a damn!

I said 'in the dark', and that is what it really was. Of course it wasn't always pitch dark, but it is hard for people living now with all the reflections across the sky from neighbouring towns to realise how truly dark it could be then. I have known cloudy nights with no moon when it was absolutely black so that one could not see one's hand in front of one's face. Sometimes, if instead of going down the lane I went over Hampton's Field to Hendy's Lane, I took a hurricane lantern with me because of the chance of walking into some cattle, but I was never very happy with it because I felt so exposed in the middle of the pool of light, and as the shadows of my legs passing one another stretched out to the circle of blackness I felt that whoever was lurking therein had the advantage of me, for they could see me whereas I could not see them.

Talking of Hampton's, it was while sitting on the stile at the bottom of the field that I had one of the most worrying experiences of my life. I got to thinking about the full implications of committing the Unforgivable Sin, which I had been told at Sunday school was the sin against the Holy Ghost. I realised I was not quite sure what that was and I had a nasty feeling that at some time or other I might have said something critical about the Holy Ghost without realising it. The possibility that I might unwittingly have done something which the Almighty would never forgive worried me for several days, but I must have got over it. Anyway, I decided that in future I would take great care to avoid that particular sin. It was while sitting on that same stile reading a 7d part of Harmsworth's Self Educator which someone had lent me that I learned the theories of Copernicus as to the movement of the planets.

Come to think of it there must have been something special about that stile. When I have time I shall have to write an article on 'Stiles I Have Known', for it has just occurred to me that of all the stiles I know, no two are alike. They all have an individuality of their own. Of course I should have to include gates too, for the next gate at the top of Hendy's Lane had a special significance for me. It was the sort of gate which swung freely. One could throw it wide open and it would swing back on its own. If, because of wet weather or for some other reason, I went that way to school, I took the opportunity of testing my luck for the day. It worked like this: I would fling the gate wide open, at the same time selecting a stick or stone in the lane a few yards away. I then made a dash for this, and if I got to it before the gate slammed behind me I knew the day would work out favourably. If on the other hand … but we won't go into that because it very rarely did. You see, I was very careful to select a mark which I felt it was within my capacity to reach.

It was during the building of a house just by the gate that I was first introduced to one of the principles on which trade unions are based. Just before six one evening I watched a labourer filling a wheelbarrow with red sandstones. He had just filled it when the whistle at the saw mills blew to signal knocking-off time, whereupon he tipped all the stones out onto the ground again. On my enquiring the reason for this he explained that it was knocking-off time, an explanation that seemed less than adequate.

At the bottom of Hendy's Lane on the right was the yard of the saw mills, and on the left the home of Dr Boodle where I spent many happy and quite a few anxious hours. Just how it came about I do not remember but the good doctor somehow found out that I was interested in literature and gave me the run of his library, occasionally inviting me to an evening meal. The anxiety arose from the fact that during dinner and after he usually questioned me on the books I had read. Some of the books were a bit beyond me and I was afraid of making a poor showing. I well remember how prior to one visit I finished reading *The Bible in Spain* by George Borrow against the clock, or rather against the watch, as I had a watch propped up in the window sill. Poor Dr Boodle. His house was furnished in excellent taste and seemed to me to be the ideal home, so much so that I once said innocently how much I envied his knowledge and his home. I was astonished and not a little bit shocked when he said, 'Don't envy me: I am very lonely. The fact is I have indulged in so much high-brow literature, music and art that in a village community like this I am the odd man out. The villagers are not interested in what I want to talk about and I am not interested in what they want to talk about, so we remain strangers to one another.' Some years later he moved to Surrey and someone sent me a newspaper cutting reporting that he had committed suicide there.

Talking of suicides reminds me of another village notability, a Mr Powell. I understand that he was the adopted son of some wealthy couple and had been to Cambridge University. He was a bachelor and came to live at Mitcheldean. His trouble was that he had no employment and no need for employment. He tried to fill in his time with hobbies and had marvellous collections of stamps, coins, birds' eggs, etc. He built Latchen Room, now the village hall, and had a museum in the basement. But these things did not really satisfy him and in an endeavour to be sociable he frequented the Yew Tree inn, where he drank whisky and treated all and sundry. He drank more and more, became more drink sodden, dirty and unkempt, and finally was found dead on the Mersey foreshore with an empty whisky bottle beside him.

These two tragedies exemplify the difficulty which middle-class people from the city experienced in retiring to the country. One must remember that at that time there were practically no motor cars to enable them to keep in touch with cultural centres. Living in a village is an art that comes naturally to those born there but is

Longhope Cricket Club in 1914. George Bullock is the umpire on the far right, and Arthur is seated in the front holding a piece of paper.

very difficult to acquire by those brought up in larger and more active communities. I could give many instances to prove this, of people who tried but just could not fit in.

It would take far too long to cover all the sights, scenes and sounds which formed the background of my childhood, but I must mention Yartleton Hill, which because of the games which took place on its summit on May Day was known as May Hill. It is of course a landmark for miles around, with its crown of fir trees planted to commemorate the 1887 Jubilee of Queen Victoria. This hill dominated Longhope. It was the hill we viewed from Hill View. The presence or absence of a cloud cap was a certain weather indicator. Its spongy springy turf was the loveliest carpet I have ever trodden upon and I can smell the pungent scent of the thyme, fern and gorse even now. It was the window on the world outside our valley – and what a window. One could see the Severn Vale, the Black Mountains in South Wales and for at least sixty miles across Herefordshire and Worcester including Bredon Hill, made famous by A.E. Housman. We had picnics galore on the summit of May Hill on national holidays, and one of my greatest joys was to lie in a grassy hollow on a windy day and let the gale shriek over the top. Incidentally, one such gale accompanied by rain occurred at the lighting of the beacon on the night of the coronation of George V. I have always felt a proprietorial right in May Hill because for over fifty years my father was the member of the Longhope Parish Council, who had special responsibility for the common land and grove of firs on the summit.

Two

Changing Times

Myself when young did eagerly frequent
Doctor and Saint, and heard great Argument
About it and about: but evermore
Came out by the same Door as in I went.

(Edward Fitzgerald, *The Ruba'iya't of Omar Khayya'm*)

The morning of 7 September 1911 at the end of that terribly hot summer found
me standing on the platform of Longhope Station in the company of 'Tib' Ellis,
Maurice Carter, Ewart Stanley and two other passengers waiting for the 7.06 a.m.
train to take me to Gloucester for my first day at Sir Thomas Rich's School. Ewart
Stanley, son of the Baptist minister, had been a pupil there for some time, but Ellis
and Carter were going to the Crypt. I had new clothes, a brand new satchel full
of books and a navy blue cap with an elaborate badge bearing the motto 'Garde
ta Foi': 'Keep Thy Promise'. I felt very self-conscious and somewhat apprehensive
at this break-out from my cosy valley. I was really suffering from an inferiority
complex (although the phrase had not yet been coined) and I remember that when
one of the other travellers asked Ewart Stanley how long the holidays had been and
he replied 'Practically seven weeks', I was amazed at the ease with which he used
the word 'practically' and wondered if I should ever be able to use such words with
equal fluency.

On arriving at the school I was given the choice of taking Latin or shorthand and
book-keeping. I chose Latin and was placed in Form 3A, which contained thirty boys
with Mr Sherwood of Grange Court as form master, the headmaster being Mr E. Price.
Coming from a village school I confess that I felt a bit lost among so many boys, none
of who I knew, and my first day was not very happy. However, it came to an end and
it was with relief that I settled in the 5 p.m. train en route for home which I reached at
about 6.15 p.m. This twelve-hour day with about two hours of homework was to be my
lot for the next three years, when by an arrangement with the headmaster I was allowed
to catch the 3.40 train on condition that I did extra homework. During the winter I
only saw Longhope in daylight at the weekends. I soon made friends and gradually settled down, and felt easier as it became apparent that I had a lot of other country boys as
fellow pupils, and that the town boys, although having a superficial slickness, were very
ordinary underneath. I also found that I could hold my own with them at almost eve-

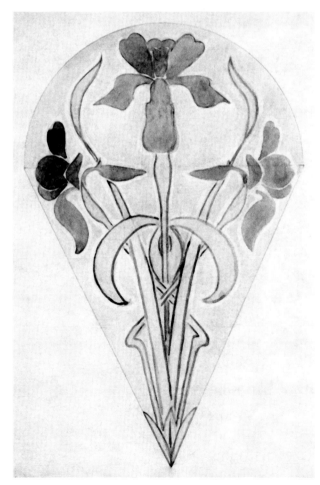

Above: Longhope railway station, where Arthur caught his daily train to school.

Left: A design of irises by Arthur from his time at Sir Thomas Rich's School. Both design and horticulture were to remain lifelong interests.

rything. This restored my confidence and, being interested in all subjects, I thoroughly enjoyed the rest of my time at school.

It may come as a surprise to learn that such was the teaching at the small out-of-date Longhope Church School that during my four years at Rich's I added nothing to my knowledge of arithmetic, and for two of those years very little to my knowledge of history and geography. You must forgive me if I indulge in a little boasting here but it is true that I was always top in maths; in fact, I never remember getting less than 90 per cent in any mathematical subject in any exam, and on one school report I had seven 'Excellent's for exams and six for work in term. I only had 'Fair' for Latin and 'Good' for French. I have already paid tribute to Mr Hill, and I should like here to pay tribute to the staff at Rich's, in spite of the fact that they must now all be dead. I would mention particularly Mr Sherwood for arithmetic, Benfield for geography, Freeman for physics, Williams for art, West for English and history, Price for advanced English and Larcombe for mathematics. Of these, West and Larcombe stand out as absolutely brilliant. Men of such ability now go where the financial rewards are greater, whereas these were dedicated schoolmasters.

Under West we took history from 1485 to modern times. We had set text books for basic reference but his method was best expressed in his own words:

> While you can learn history from reading and pictures, the best way to understand and memorise it is to analyse it and write it down in your own words. History is made up of movements of groups of people, some in sequence, some overlapping, some big, some small, but having three things in common – causes, events and results. We will try and distinguish these movements and write down our findings under the three headings – Causes, Events, Results.

Then we started to write notes and we nearly all got 'writer's cramp', but as a result my best friend Blatchford was first in history in all England in the Cambridge examination.

But Larcombe … He was the master teacher par excellence. When he was our form master in Form 6 he was a BSc, but he later became known to thousands as Dr Larcombe, writer of many books on mathematics. Looking back I suppose he, more than any other person, influenced my way of looking at things. He insisted that nothing can be taken for granted. Where a thing can be proved it must be proved; and where it can't be proved the verdict must be on the balance of evidence for or against until further proof comes to light. His method was not to be a teacher talking down to his pupils from a lofty platform of superior knowledge, but he stepped down amongst them to act as a trained guide. As an example of this I remember him saying once when we were going through some previous examination papers:

> These papers contain geometrical riders which are capable of temporarily flooring anybody. If I wanted to impress you I could have acquainted myself with the solutions beforehand and slapped them on the board, but that would not have helped you very much. Instead of that we will solve them together. We will go through them step by step and if I get stuck, instead of sniggering behind my back I want your suggestions. You watch me get out of the difficulties and you might one day learn how to get out of them yourself.

The Choir and East Window ('Crécy Window') of Gloucester Cathedral, from *The Story of Gloucester Cathedral*, by G.H. Cook (Phoenix House, London, 1952).

In 1914 the First World War broke out, and some months later Larcombe, who was the assistant headmaster, headed a group of teachers who thought it their duty to join up. Mr Price, the headmaster, was opposed to this, but they had their way and four of them were killed in action. They were replaced by lady teachers, but I'm afraid they were not of the same calibre, nor could the boys be persuaded to take them seriously. The result was a falling-off in standards. I was a bit sorry for them, especially on one occasion for Miss Hayes, a very attractive young French teacher. Prior to one of her lessons Bob Manning, the son of a stage comedian and a comedian in his own right, who sat in the front row, distributed electric snuff to all the boys in class with instructions that when he took out his handkerchief everyone was to take a pinch. At the same time he lightly powdered the top of the teacher's desk. Miss Hayes came in and the lesson started: the handkerchief came out and the snuff was taken. Sneezing commenced all over the room. Miss Hayes ordered that sneezing should stop and threatened to send the next sneezer to the headmaster, but banging the desk brought up the snuff on the lid and she started sneezing herself. The air was filled with snuff and sneezing. Then she started to cry and ran for the headmaster. He came quickly and 'read the Riot Act'. We all had to apologise to Miss Hayes and Bob Manning received what he expected.

The war curtailed our sporting activities but I played soccer for the school and captained the Country House at cricket. I took the Cambridge Junior Examination in Form V and passed comfortably, though not as well as I should have done; but I did not take the Senior Cambridge. I believe my parents said there was no point in it as there was no question of my going to a university and they wanted me to start work – all much to the disappointment of Mr Price, who would have liked to see me read law.

One interesting point about the Cambridge Junior Examination was that it was taken in the chapter house of Gloucester Cathedral and as I took my history paper there I thought what better place than on the spot where William the Conqueror ordered Domesday Book to be compiled in December 1085? Another interesting event which took place while at Rich's was my confirmation by special arrangement with Bishop Gibson – right in front of the 'Crécy' window, more or less on the spot where Henry III was crowned with an iron ring. Later, in the Army, I marched across the Crécy battlefield, and for a time after the Armistice in 1918 I was in charge of a guard post on the south bank of the Somme, almost exactly where Edward III with the Black Prince and the English Army crossed the river prior to the battle.

It is hard to convey to anyone born after, say, 1908, the essence of living before 4 August 1914. In this connection it is worthwhile recording part of a conversation which took place between my daughter Nancy and myself one Sunday morning on 4 August many years later. She was only a little girl and we were lying in adjoining bedrooms with the doors open while my wife was preparing breakfast.

'Ah,' I said, ruminating, 'this is the anniversary of the day the world changed.'

'Oh,' she answered, 'What day was that?'

I replied, 'August 4th 1914,' and added, 'On that day something went out of the world, and will never come back.'

She said, 'What was it?' This rather put me on the spot and for the life of me I didn't know. Her response was somewhat crushing: 'Well if you don't know you ought not to have mentioned it, as I wasn't born then.'

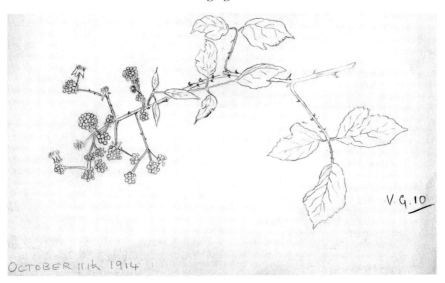

OCTOBER 11th 1914

These two drawings from Arthur's school days hint at the poignancy of the First World War generation: the young man who did the delicate study of a bramble was also sufficiently incensed about German militarism to create this strongly satirical image.

Since then I've thought a lot about it and come to the conclusion that one of the things which vanished or nearly vanished was genuine 'fun'. Life suddenly became sophisticated and smart. Not only was the quantity of laughter greatly reduced, but it lost its quality, and the tendency to synthetic jollity has, I believe, been accentuated by the advent of radio and television. As society has become more affluent and 'educated', it seems to me that there has been less and less genuine spontaneous gaiety. There are of course many exceptions, but most people seem to be putting on an act in the frantic endeavour to be 'with it'.

But I must go back to 4 August because it is surrounded with so many pictures which became etched on my memory. My brother, Wallace, had left Longhope for the Eldorado of the south Wales coalfield and was working as a labourer at Glyncorrwg Colliery for four times the wages he could get at Longhope as a skilled craftsman. He was living in the mining village of Blaengwynfi and playing in the band. In an unexpected burst of generosity he invited my sister Lucy and me (then fourteen) to stay with him for a few days. We did, and one Saturday descended from the Rhondda Valley, Port Talbot and Swansea Bay train at Blaengwynfi station. Outside the station was a small coal tip and on top of it was a galvanised iron shed from which emanated strains of excellent music. The band was engaged in its weekly practice. I only realised later how much of an escape from their sordid surroundings music – either vocal or instrumental – meant to the people of the industrial valleys of South Wales. And sordid they were, with a peculiar smell which penetrated the houses, the Workmen's Hall and the chapels – a smell which I have never got out of my nostrils and which I found was common to all the mining valleys I afterwards visited. It may be interesting to note that the railway station many years later became – temporarily – 'Blaenavon' in the filming of J. Cronin's story *The Citadel*.

The next day being Sunday, we decided to go to church. This was situated in Abergwynfi, a twin village just across a shallow stream. It was a lovely day with the sun streaming through the windows, and the preacher was the chaplain of Cardiff gaol. As he looked round on the tiny congregation he must have wondered whether a sermon was justified, poor man. I expect he has been dead many years, but he might have been encouraged if he had known that the ginger-headed boy halfway down the church who didn't appear to be taking any notice would be quoting something he said fifty-eight years later. That something struck me as very profound. He explained that nobody had any alibis for wrongdoing and that 'We all know it's right to do right'.

The next day was August Bank Holiday, 4 August. This too was a lovely summer day and we spent it on Aberavon sands. As we left we bought an evening newspaper to learn that England had declared war on Germany.

There was a lot of joking about it and the general view was that it would only last a few weeks with Germany crushed between France and the Russian steamroller. There was no suggestion of Wallace joining up; on the contrary. You can imagine our surprise, therefore, when in the middle of September (after we had returned home) a postcard was received from Shrewsbury to say that he was now a private in the King's Shropshire Light Infantry. The next time we saw him he was in a temporary navy blue uniform and had spent some time drilling (with walking sticks in lieu of non-existent rifles) on Salisbury Plain. His clothes were filled with lice, which none of us had ever seen or heard of before. However, a bath and Keating's Powder soon restored him to something like normal.

It was about this time I was waiting with others on Longhope railway station for the train bringing the *Gloucester Citizen* in. It came, and in the stop press was the announcement that, somewhere near Le Cateau in north France, British and German troops had fired on one another for the first time in history.

This period saw not only the break-up of the world but of my family. Before I deal with that, however, I had better bring the family history up to date. Alice had married her childhood sweetheart, Harry Hall; Wallace was in south Wales until he joined up; Floss and Lucy were in domestic service; and, in spite of strong opposition from my parents, Ruth married Jack Daunter.

Alice's marriage was quite an event in the village. Harry Hall was very popular, not only as a first-class cricketer and footballer – he was much liked just for himself. His father, who had been the village wheelwright, had died when Harry was young. He himself worked at Constance's saw mills as a wood-turner, and the very prosperous family business (building carts, traps and wagons) was carried on by his older brother Fred (also a footballer and also very popular, especially with my sister Lucy, who I am sure would have married him – but that's a very sad story).

For the wedding everybody who was anybody in the village turned up and crowded the newly-built Latchen Room (a wedding group hung on its walls for at least twenty years after). The wedding breakfast was something to behold, and I looked forward with joyous anticipation to partaking of my share. Alas, I had none of it for, by one of those extraordinary coincidences which have dogged me all my life, I had an attack of ramping toothache and had to go home – missing the feast and the revelries.

Three other small incidents in connection with the wedding have remained in my memory. One was that, of all the family, I was the only one who had to walk to church; another was that one of the horse-drawn carriages – the one to convey the happy couple – overturned as it was turning round in the orchard (before anyone got into it, I am glad to say); and finally there were birds flying round in the church during the ceremony. Many people took note of these two latter incidents and regarded them as bad omens, which they proved to be, for although Alice and Harry were very happy this happiness was short-lived. First living in the Old Mill, they moved to Olive Villa, and while there, during a football match with Minsterworth in which he was playing in goal, Harry was accidentally but severely kicked in the groin by G. Harvey, brother of the 'Gloucestershire Poet', E. Harvey, who was also playing. An abscess developed which would not heal, in spite of treatment in bed. Harry was removed to Gloucester Royal Infirmary, where he got worse and finally died aged twenty-seven. All the time he was there he was in an advanced state of tuberculosis, which the doctors had not been able to diagnose until just before death! I visited him several times. He knew he was going to die, and didn't complain, but once he made a remark that struck me as particularly poignant: 'I sha'n't know if we won the war.'

He died about 2 a.m. with Alice at his bedside, and immediately after death took place she was asked to leave, being turned out into the street with nowhere to go, in spite of the fact that by personal gifts and organising social functions Harry had raised hundreds of pounds for that infirmary.

The sequel takes the form of another coincidence, for in 1918 my battalion relieved the 2/5th Glosters in a German strongpoint in France called Junction Post, and it so happened that I found and identified the body of Captain G. Harvey, who was killed in capturing that post.

I can't remember how it came about, but for a time Harry was confined to bed at Hill View, and I'm afraid my mother was cruelly unsympathetic. Although it was entirely contrary to Harry's nature, I think she believed him to be malingering. Matters were made worse by the birth of a son, Francis Henry, who nearly died of starvation because he could not keep down any food. His screaming was most distressing, until the doctors decided he had lost the lining to his stomach, which was only restored by a diet mainly of white of egg.

When Harry died Alice and Frank were living at Olive Villa. In a desperate effort to ensure that Frank did not die of TB she left him out in the severest weather. It must have worked for he is alive today[3]. Mother stayed and slept at Olive Villa on many occasions, and what with that and the time she had devoted to Alice at Hill View my father began to get annoyed. For her part, Mother accused him of neglect of the home, consorting with other women and drinking too much. Finally, she left home never to return. I was going daily to Gloucester and just used the house to sleep in. The doors were left unlocked. Sometimes my father did not sleep in the house, but I did not know when. I often entered the house and went to bed in the dark. I did not know if my father was in bed or indeed if there was anyone else in the house, but when morning came, he was always there to cook my breakfast.

Alice was left with very little money, and in order to live she sold Olive Villa and took a flat near Pitville Gates in Cheltenham, where she set up a dressmaking business. She was a first-class cook and needlewoman. The going was very hard indeed, and war rationing made it difficult for her to get proper food for Frank and herself, but she managed to build up an exclusive clientele. How long she could have carried on I don't know, for the poor food, long hours and close work were visibly affecting her health, but she had a very good friend named Mrs Walcroft who ran a very successful high-class boarding house in the Promenade (later part of the Municipal Offices). She was aware of Alice's capabilities and also knew that Floss (perhaps I should say Florence), who was then employed as a parlour maid at Lagorie, Eldorado Road, wished to get out of domestic service. She therefore proposed that they become partners and take over No. 4 Pitville Lawn as a high-class boarding house. She would put up the capital as a loan which they would pay back as they could. This wonderful opportunity was accepted. The business was duly established, and prospered.

This was a very unsettled period for me. The family was breaking up. Most of my friends had joined the Army or left Longhope. Recreational facilities and entertainments had been reduced to a minimum, and just for good measure I was often being insulted in the street by passing soldiers holding out their rifles to me or people asking me why I was not in the Army – all because I was rather big for my age. They did not know that I had actually enlisted at the old Labour Exchange in Southgate Street in March 1916 when I was sixteen years of age, but was not allowed to join up because I was underage. Altogether I was not very happy.

Although I cannot remember the exact date my mother left Hill View I well remember presiding over the meeting at which my parents decided to part. Mother absolutely refused to have a legal separation so I was in a weak position bargaining with my father on her behalf. The maximum I could get him to agree to was 3/– a week, and I was very apprehensive about how she was going to exist. When I joined the Army I arranged for half my pay of 7/– a week to be paid to her, but 6/6 a week to live on was ridiculous even in those days.

This very unpleasant meeting must have taken place before I joined up, and yet I am sure Mother was present on the morning I left. Anyway it was not long before she had a room near Alice in Cheltenham, furnished with some of the furniture from Hill View, and there she stayed till I left the Army in January 1920, giving Alice an occasional helping hand at the boarding house, for she was a marvellous housewife.

I have often thought it rather odd and unfortunate that it fell to me – by far the youngest member of the family – to arrange the terms of my parents' parting, but I suppose it had to be. I saw the qualities and faults of both and got on equally well with both. Although he was fond of Alice, Lucy and myself were the only two my father would seriously listen to, and Lucy was not available. It was all very sad, but inevitable. They were both splendid people in their way (I have never met or heard of anyone with a better, more balanced brain than my father), but they were just not on the same wavelength, and they were stubborn beyond belief.

It may seem an odd thing to say, but although much the youngest of the family I have felt the oldest and most responsible member since I was about seventeen.

Three

The Army

Twilight and evening bell,
And after that the dark:
And may there be no sadness of farewell
When I embark

(Alfred, Lord Tennyson, *Crossing the Bar*)

Immediately after my eighteenth birthday I left Hill View in the morning, supposedly to visit Alice in Cheltenham. I had no intention of visiting Alice, nor did I do so. Instead I went straight to the recruiting office in the Promenade and asked to be allowed to join up there and then. The actual minimum age for acceptance was eighteen years and one month, but I persuaded them to waive this, and a couple of hours later I was in the train with another recruit en route for Horfield Barracks, Bristol. I never went back to Hill View to sleep except for one night under special circumstances.

The other recruit in the railway carriage was about thirty-five, and very crude indeed. I wondered why he had not been called up before, but there he was and I sent up a silent prayer that my comrades of the future would have a little more appeal. I must confess that, having taken the plunge, I began to feel somewhat nervous about what the immediate future had in store for me – for you must realise that I had led a very free if somewhat sheltered life up till then. I had no idea what the Army was like. The nearest I had ever got to it was in the Boy Scouts.

I was soon to learn. I shall never forget walking through the gates of Horfield Barracks on to the parade ground, where squads of recruits were being drilled. I stood spellbound watching a bull-like sergeant who looked as though he would burst with the ferocity of his commands, one of which I was sure was not in any English dictionary, but which turned out to be 'Attention!' I learned this through the agonising experience of being drilled by the same sergeant during the next two or three days. Other commands were equally incomprehensible until one had (in ignorance of the meaning) chanced to disobey them.

I was allotted to a barrack room and a bed. The room was long, light and spotlessly clean with tables and benches down the centre and beds consisting of two low trestles, three boards to lay on them, a very hard mattress and three blankets. Tea was served in enamelled mugs, with thick chunks of bread, cheese and butter and (astonishingly) radishes, which had apparently just been pulled out of the barracks garden and had some earth still on them. I tried to size up my fellow recruits but had little to say to any of them. They seemed a pretty mixed lot. There was nothing to complain about, but the general impression was that of 'hardness'. I think I slept alright that night but with a lot of question marks chasing one another through my brain.

The next day (about 15 August 1917) was spent on various 'fatigues' which included scrubbing the barrack room floor with hard brushes with long handles and bristles about a third of an inch long. Uniforms and kit were also given out and our private clothes were packed in parcels and sent home. I wondered if I should ever see mine again. Food was coarse but wholesome and reasonably plentiful.

So far so good, but then there was the parade ground, and I am bound to say that our welcome there was daunting to say the least. We were made up into squads, under drill sergeants who soon made it clear that between them and us friendship or mercy was impossible. This apparent hatred of us and everything connected with us was so great that they were determined to work us into the ground, and that hatred was only equalled by their contempt for our physique, our general intelligence and our ability to become guardsmen instantaneously. Their remarks about our origin and ancestry were distinctly uncomplimentary, and when they stated that before they had finished with us we should wish our mothers had never borne us, cold shivers went down my back. Their treatment of the English language was most fascinating, but I soon learned how to translate it, so that when I heard a noise like a strangled hippopotamus

Arthur was recruited as a volunteer, aged eighteen, to the serve in the First World War. He served as a Lewis gunner on the Front Line for the 2/4th 'Ox & Bucks' Light Infantry, and later for the 2/5th Gloucestershire Regiment.

shouting 'Sl–i–i–i–p–Ips!' I knew I was being requested to slope arms, which of course I did. I realised that these sergeants could not be quite as inhuman as they sounded, and soon learned that most of them were quite decent chaps and that this was just their jolly way of conditioning us to become automata.

We only stayed at Horfield long enough to learn elementary drill and to be sorted out for various training camps. In a few days about 200 of us went by train to Chiseldon Camp on Salisbury Plain just outside Swindon. Although this was a big hutted camp, it was very overcrowded. We were allotted to F Company of the 35th Training Reserve Battalion, nominally part of the Devon Regiment. When you realise that a normal battalion consists of four companies, A, B, C and D, and totals between 800 and 1,000 men, you will gather that the 35th Training Reserve was somewhat unwieldy, having six companies, one of which, F, contained some 800 recruits.

We arrived in the middle of a very hot day, and were handed over to a corporal who proceeded to give us a lurid lecture on 'venereal disease' and its perils, with special reference to Swindon, which apparently made Sodom and Gomhorra seem like a rest home for Plymouth Brethren. The lecture ending, we were led to the dining hut, which had already seen two relays of hungry recruits. Enamelled plates and mugs were on the tables, the former containing dregs of tea and the latter traces of stew and fish bones. Bones and chewed bits of gristle were all over the tables. We sat down, and the cooks came in with huge cans of stew. This was sploshed from ladles onto the dirty plates before us, and that was dinner. If you were really hungry you ate it and if you didn't eat it you weren't really hungry. That's all there was to it. An orderly officer with sergeant came round and asked if there were any complaints. One recruit innocently stood up and commenced his complaint. He didn't get far before he was stopped and put on a charge of insolence to an officer.

The huts were overcrowded to bursting point so we had to sleep on the floor of the guard room without beds or blankets. Unfortunately the door kept blowing open, which allowed admittance to a great St Bernard dog – the mascot of the camp. This confounded dog would lie down by me and snore, so I had no sleep that night.

Next day a big draft left the camp, which made it possible for us to be allotted to huts and beds, but all the time I was there Chiseldon was a very 'rough house' in every way. Just to illustrate what I mean I must refer again to the dining huts. These were on a slope and had about three steps up to the doors at the lower end. On either side of the steps was tangled barbed wire to force orderly entry up the steps, and the doors were always locked. Because of the relays of diners, soldiers tried to be first in the queue. Soon there was a crowd fighting to get in. Every day the doors were crushed in, the barbed wire trampled flat and some one injured as the hungry mass exploded into the hut. Every day the doors and wire were restored and every day I was there the performance was repeated. I only put my foot on the steps two or three times at dinner time.

It was at Chiseldon that I first realised the effect of uniform as a leveller, but only as a leveller so far as the outside veneer is concerned. Socially all privates were equal, but once the outside trappings were removed the only differences remaining were the qualities of the man. And what a mixed lot we were. It wasn't long before I had struck up a friendship with three people of first-class calibre, two of whom remained as close friends nearly till the Armistice, one well after. First there was Lance Corporal

Johnson, educated at King Edward's Grammar School, Birmingham, and who later was house surgeon at Queen's Hospital, Birmingham. Then Barnard, who belonged to a well-known Gloucester family. His father was managing director of Waite James, a firm of grain importers. One of his brothers was Major Barnard, who commanded the 7th Glosters in Mesopotamia, and another brother had been killed as a lance corporal in the Tank Corps. Finally, Osmond. He too had a good education, came of a good Bristol family, very lovable but very naive and impractical. After the war he joined his brother in running a nursery at Wickwar.

I met all of them separately in civilian life after the war, just by chance. Johnson then was Dr Johnson, with a big medical practice in Birmingham. Barnard was heavyweight boxing champion of Birmingham University, and Osmond was in the horticultural business. All three were absolutely fearless. Johnson and Barnard were quite outstanding. Neither put on an act, but both were prepared to stand on their own two feet and take on anybody at nearly anything. I'll tell you more about Barnard later, but the following episode involving Johnson will illustrate what I mean by my last sentence.

I think it was at Rollestone that Johnson occupied the end bed as lance-corporal, and, believe it or not, he always knelt down at his bedside and prayed before going to sleep. I have never heard of anyone else doing such a thing in the Army. Usually there was some sniggering but no interference, but on one occasion several fellows who had perhaps had a drink too much started cat-calling, and one threw a boot at him. He took no notice till he had finished his prayers. He then walked up the hut (containing about thirty men) and asked who threw the boot. Nobody answered, but it was obvious who the culprit was. He was sitting on his bed. Johnson told him to get up. As he still sat, Johnson took him by the top of his shirt and yanked him to his feet. Johnson told him to get down on his knees and apologise, or put his fists up to defend himself. He did neither, so Johnson gave him one almighty swipe on the jaw and knocked him cold. Then turning to the hut he said if anybody else wanted the same treatment they could have it. He always said his prayers in peace thereafter.

That was one thing I liked about the Army. Broadly speaking there was no double talk. If you thought a man a fool or a liar you said so and took whatever consequences there were.

Was I thankful when the news came that some of us were being transferred to Fovant, near Salisbury. The officer in command there was a giant colonel now fairly old, who had been a famous big game hunter. When he saw us on our first parade he remarked that we looked half-starved and needed feeding up. And they did feed us up. Fovant was as good a camp as Chiseldon was a bad one, and that is saying a lot. Those of us who wished to were even allowed to skip early parade (6 a.m. to 7.30 a.m.) and do cross-country running in lieu – for which running gear was provided.

Speaking of Fovant reminds me of something which I think mildly amusing. I must explain that most of us young soldiers were always very hungry and could eat almost anything. But there was one item which very few could stomach and that was rissoles. It was known that these brown lumps were composed of scraps and leftovers from other meals. Therefore when rissoles appeared on the breakfast tables nearly everybody got up and left. The real rissole-wallahs remained for the great feast of the week. This happened one day at Fovant, and I can see now in my mind's eye the big dining hut with hundreds of enamelled plates each with a rissole on it and about ten seated soldiers, all of whom burst out into self-conscious laughter before setting to! But even we couldn't eat them all!

It couldn't last. In the Army everybody is always moving on somewhere. Apparently the Australians at Rollestone Camp (an offshoot of Lark Hill) were finding it a bit too bleak. Several had died from exposure – no wonder, as they were too drunk to get back to camp – and they were coming to the milder climate of Fovant. So we went to Rollestone in the autumn of 1917. I must confess it really was a bit bleak there, and for a short time, about Christmas, all taps were frozen, water coming by water cart. One night our corrugated iron cinema was blown off its foundations and found as a crumpled mass about a mile away.

While at Rollestone we learnt that there was an outbreak of spotted fever (meningitis) among New Zealanders at Sling Camp, with a death rate of 50 per cent. So the authorities decided to 'swab' a proportion of the men in each unit on the plain. In our battalion one platoon in every company was swabbed (i.e. 25 per cent). My platoon was one of these. A few days later I was firing on the miniature range when an orderly came shouting my name. I was ordered to go back to the hut, collect my toothbrush and shaving kit, and report to the battalion office. There I found three other men, as puzzled as I was as to why we were there. Then I was informed that an ambulance was taking us to hospital at Tidworth. I protested that there must be some mistake as I was feeling very well indeed. But it had no effect, and off we went.

At Tidworth we were allotted to the married quarters, with two rooms up, two down and the necessary offices[4]. We were given blue hospital uniforms and forbidden to contact any other soldiers or civilians. Each day breakfast would be delivered, together with meat and vegetables, bread etc., with which we would cook all other meals. All scraps and refuse was to be burned. You can assume that this was very puzzling and alarming, and that alarm was not reduced when we were informed that our swabs had shown positive meningitis and we were under strict isolation. But the alarm was equalled by our relief when it was decided (after cross-examination) that we could not have active meningitis and were only 'carriers' who might have had the germs since birth. As carriers we could not develop the disease itself, though we could pass it to others under certain conditions. So we were to attend a fumigating room for a period each day until tests showed three negatives. Within a week I was back at Rollestone, but in the meantime we had a jolly good time lazing about, reading, writing and playing cards. The amount of food was such that we had to institute the six-meal day, so when we left we were well set up to stand the rigours of that very cold camp.

Lark Hill held about 250,000 troops when I was there and resembled an American Western mushroom town in nearly all respects. But we didn't stay long, and off we went to billets off the Magdalen Road in Norwich.

Norwich appealed to me as a very interesting city. Troops were billeted everywhere, sleeping on mattresses on the floors of the front rooms of the terraced houses – three men to a house – and using local schools and halls as mess rooms. Billets were quite comfortable and the people did all they could to help us, even to the point of supplementing our very poor food from their own meagre rations. It was odd how the food varied from place to place, but Norwich was very bad. On one occasion a mouse's nest, complete with mice, was served up in some (boiled) dried cod.

Arthur before going to France to serve in the First World War, aged eighteen years old.

The chief thing I remember about military life in Norwich was the shocking and apparently incurable truancy. Parades were held in the streets. Roll call as usual was at 6 a.m. and of course it was dark at that time in January. The numbers appearing on parade got noticeably fewer and fewer each day, yet nearly every name called on the roll was answered. At last it became ridiculous. One morning only about fifteen men were present out of about 200 but the names were being replied to as called, until one man answered 'present' to about twenty names straight off. Then the balloon really did go up. Officers and NCOs made a systematic search of every billet, but the alarm had been raised and few absentees could be found. The civilians in the billets entered into the game. Soldiers were hidden in WCs and under the beds in private bedrooms (where the officers could not go) and in fact wherever anyone could be hidden.

It is true that following this scare numbers on parade went up, but they were only normal on battalion or other special parades. We frequently drilled on Moushold Heath, famous for its connection with Jack Cade's rebellion. Occasionally night operations took place there. The battalion would parade in the dark and march to the heath, with NCOs on each side carrying lanterns to prevent men dropping out of the column. But it was no use. Invariably it arrived at the heath sadly depleted, many of the absentees having found their way to the cinemas in Norwich or a local pub.

I must say I enjoyed my stay in Norwich, and it might be worth recording that I sang on six occasions in the choir of Norwich Cathedral. During our stay in Norwich, men with the necessary standard of education were invited to apply for commissions in the Royal Flying Corps or the Infantry. I was one of several who submitted an application, and so was an acquaintance called Pike, whom I met later on in France under most remarkable circumstances. Pike and two or three more were transferred for officer training, but the posting of the rest of us had not come through before Ludendorff made his tremendous effort to break the Allied line on 21 March 1918.

About this time we were scheduled for leave, and the passes and rail vouchers had been issued, when the War Office cancelled all leave. Men were asked to return passes etc., but as they realised they might never see their people again, they point blank refused to do so. After a lot of fuss they were allowed to proceed, but when I got to my sister Alice's house at 4 Pitville Lawn, Cheltenham, which I then regarded as home, there was a telegram awaiting me, ordering me to return to Norwich.

So after a few hours I said goodbye to Mother and Alice and left for the station. Fortunately, as I went up the stairs from the basement on the way to the front door, I stumbled up the stairs. Mother exclaimed 'That means good luck', and the tension was ended by a laugh.

Arriving at Norwich we immediately left for Southampton, and at 8 p.m. on 1 April I found myself complete with full equipment, including two blankets, among thousands of troops going aboard the SS *Viper*. As I took my second foot off the quay to walk up the gangway I sent up a silent prayer that it might not be the last time I stood on English soil.

Four

'Dix Chevaux ou Cinquante Hommes'

And you, good yeomen,
Whose limbs were made in England, show us here
The mettle of your pasture.

(William Shakespeare, Henry V)

The SS *Viper* joined an enormous fleet which was assembling in the Solent in evening sunlight. Long grey destroyers were going to and fro and signalling with light to one another and to the shore. Darkness fell, and the convoy started for France. Curtains were pulled down by the sailors from one deck to another, and all lights were obscured, except on the destroyers, which tore round the outside of the fleet, sweeping the sea with their searchlights in search of German U-boats.

What a voyage. I assume that every ship was packed as full as we were, but I can only describe conditions aboard the *Viper*, if that is possible. I stayed on the deck, which was crowded, but I knew it would be more crowded below. I had to go below once, and that was enough. All the floors, corridors, WCs and urinals were covered with men lying in all directions and all postures. One could not step between them so one just had to walk on them. The stench of sweat, vomit, beer and urine was simply dreadful, and the air was almost solid with 'fug'. I was astonished that nobody was suffocated, but when daylight came and we found ourselves safely in harbour at Le Havre, there they were all merry and bright.

The harbour was packed with ships. Between the SS *Viper* and the quay were two ships alongside one another, which we had to cross to land. Having landed we formed up and marched to a canvas camp on the hills behind St Adresse (a suburb of Le Havre). The distance to the camp was three or four miles. When we got there we were allotted fifteen men to a bell tent, which meant that some had to sleep outside. We only stayed the night before marching down to Le Havre to entrain for Rouen and the Front.

At the station our train awaited us. It consisted of covered vans with a sliding door on each side, and painted on the side were the words 'Dix chevaux ou cinquante hommes' – ten horses or fifty men. They were always referred to as cattle trucks, but I doubt if any cattle ever went in them. Whoever decided they could carry fifty men was an optimist or a sadist. The lucky ones sat on the floor with their backs against the side or end, and, of course, the rest in the middle, but after some hours of travel the sitters slept and

H.M.S Lion going into action.

This drawing from Arthur's schooldays shows HMS *Lion* going into action. It illustrates the type of ship in use at the time, and also that the war was an important issue for him from the very beginning.

slumped on to the floor in one jumbled mass, and it was a little off-putting to wake up and find a pair of army boots on one's face. We arrived at Rouen on 3 April, and after an uncomfortable stay under canvas we entrained for the front on the 6th.

During our stay in Rouen some 400 of us were posted to the 2/4th Oxfordshire and Buckinghamshire Light Infantry, and we were issued with our identity discs, of a kind of plastic, about 2in in diameter, with name and number impressed thereon and a piece of string attached with which to hang it around one's neck. They were very important, but for some reason or other they could not be distributed individually before we left, so when our draft of about 500 strong (nearly all eighteen or nineteen years old) paraded to depart, a bag containing the discs was handed to a soldier, who was told to carry it a bit and then pass it on to someone else. It was not very heavy, but you must realise that we were in full kit, weighing about 60lb, with two rolled blankets on the top, and this was onerous on a long march.

We set off, and before long the disc carrier passed on his bag successfully. This occurred two or three times and then stopped, as no one else would take the bag. The man carrying it got really fed up, and at last he said, 'To hell with this', and dumped it in the gutter. I often wondered what became of it, but there certainly was some row when we reached our battalion without them.

Before we leave Rouen I should mention that it was here I first heard the guns: a faint but continuous rumble, and that sound never ceased until 11 November 1918, though it is true that it sometimes decreased to a kind of a mutter.

As we slowly – very slowly – chugged along to our unknown fate, with legs dangling out of the doors on both sides of the truck, everybody was in high spirits and a few took pot shots with their rifles at whatever took their fancy in the landscape until stopped by the officers. At last we reached a small place called Hangest sur Somme. The train stopped and we descended. There in front of us was a muddy, sluggish and

FLANDERS

January 1916

A card sent home by Arthur's elder brother, Wallace, in 1916, jesting about the amount of kit carried by the 20th Light Division.

somewhat narrow stream, which has given its name to one of the most awful battles in history – the Somme.

The rumble of the guns was now very heavy and ominous, and one could even pick out the firing of the really big guns. It was getting dusk. We were given bully beef and biscuits; and though the grass was wet with rain we sat on the riverbank and ate them. It was not a very good meal but we were very hungry, having had nothing to eat since breakfast at 5 a.m.

APRIL, 1918.

Friday 5

Still in camp. Transferred to 2/4th.
Ox + Bucks. Light Inf. No. 34336

Saturday 6

5 p.m. leave Rouen for unit Arrive Hangest
5.30 p.m. No food since breakfast. 6.30 tea
finished, start night march through rain
darkness and mud. Fellows almost riot.
Arrive brigade headquarters 12.30 a.m.
Turn in wet through on sodden roadside.

Low Sunday. Sunday 7

6 a.m. March 3 miles on to billets to find them full
Remain in village till 8 a.m. Breakfast
of tea and dear. Leave village 2 p.m.
Arrive Hancourt 5 miles distance at 4.30 p.m
Billeted in barns.

Memo.

Entries in Arthur's diary for 6 and 7 April 1918, recording his arrival in Hangest-sur-Somme and the gruelling march to Hancourt.

After tea about 6.30 p.m. we formed up and started to march. It was soon dark, and the only light was from the flashes of the guns near Amiens. It started to rain heavily, and we were soon wet through; our packs and the rolled blankets on top of them were like lead. At the end of fifty minutes we took the usual break of ten minutes, and so it went on, hour after hour. Sometimes we seemed to go towards the line and sometimes away from it.

What with the darkness, the rain and the weight we were carrying, plus the growing conviction that whoever was guiding us was completely lost, men became bad tempered and exhausted, so that after three or four hours the formation was broken and we just straggled along, with the line growing longer and longer. There were two or three officers riding up and down on horses, exhorting men to keep up, but it was useless. They just couldn't. When the hourly order to halt passed down the line, men just pitched forward, or sideways, into the swilling mud on the road and were asleep before they hit the ground. Nor could they be roused to go on again – or only with very great difficulty. At last, at between 2 and 3 a.m., after about eight hours marching in torrential rain, whoever was in charge decided it was hopeless going on (even if we knew where we were going), as practically everybody was utterly exhausted, so the message was passed down that we would halt till daylight. Most men lay strewn about the road, but a few of us just had enough strength left to creep off into a cornfield where the shoots were 5 or 6in long. The soil was just soft mud. The only waterproof thing we had was a rubber ground sheet about 30in wide by about 5ft long. I decided that I would rather use it to keep the rain off than lie on it, so I just lay cradled in soft mud with wet grass against my face and went to sleep.

When dawn came – I suppose about 6.30 a.m. – we were roused by officers and sergeants, who told us there was a small village just along the road and we were to make our way to it. Fortunately the rain stopped and the sun came out. I remembered it was Sunday. We got to the village, which was a very poor one with mud and wattle walls, and there tried to dry and clean ourselves up. There was no food available, but a field kitchen had been secured from somewhere, plus some tea, so we all had a hot drink of tea – minus milk and sugar – and were very thankful for that small mercy.

It took a long time for the stragglers to come in, but by 2 p.m. we were sufficiently rested to move on, and that we did until about 4 o'clock in the afternoon when we reached our destination, the village of Hancourt, near Warlus. Here we joined the twenty-two survivors of the 2/4th Battalion of the Oxfordshire and Buckinghamshire Light Infantry, belonging to the 184th Brigade of the 61st Division. Apart from the battalion transport (which was not in the line) these were the sole survivors of the battalion. They had between them, except for their clothes, one rifle and three sets of webbing equipment. I doubt if in the whole war any battalion was wiped out so completely.

To understand this it is necessary to remember that on 21 March 1918 the German armies, under Hindenberg and Ludendorff, made one last desperate and tremendous effort to break through the Allied line. I won't go into a lot of detail, but the place chosen was the right flank of the 5th Army where it joined the French. The attack was probably the most concentrated in history, for in the space of a few days 106 divisions, totalling over two million men, were thrown into battle on a fifty mile front. The absolute spearhead of this attack was the road going due west out of St Quentin. One of the survivors, named Twigg (or Twiggin), told me that the Ox. & Bucks were entrenched right across that road and he actually occupied a post dug right in the middle of it!

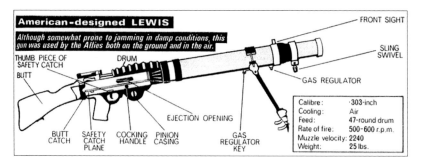

The Lewis gun, which Arthur was to use in action. From *A Military Atlas of the First World War* by Arthur Banks (Pen and Sword Books)

What happened is set out in *The Story of the 2/5th Gloucestershire Regiment* (one of the three battalions forming the 184th Brigade), but I quote some extracts which will explain why only twenty-two survived.

First, from the War Despatch of Sir Ivor Maxse, commanding the 18th Corps:

2/8th Worcesters, 2/4th Oxfords and Bucks, and a 2/5th Gordon Highlanders were holding a front of 6,000 yards and occupied ground to a depth of 1,500 yards in rear of their outposts. These heroic battalions were first subjected to an intensive bombardment by all calibres of guns and trench mortars for five hours and were then overwhelmed by not less than three German divisions which assaulted at 10 a.m. The fog prevented SOS rockets from being seen and so prevented the artillery and machine-gun section from co-operating by firing on distant targets. The Redoubt remained in telephonic communication with Corps Headquarters by means of a buried cable till 4.10 p.m. At that hour the garrisons were told that they might cut their way out at night, but except for a few odd men no one returned from the three battalions whose duty it was to hold the Forward Zone. They simply fought it out on the spot and their heroism will live for ever in the annals of their regiments … Details are lacking but we know that they held up three divisions throughout the whole day and prevented the enemy from assaulting the Battle Zone of the 61st Division.[5]

Secondly, Major General Colin Mackenzie, commanding the 61st Division:

[These] Redoubts in the Forward Zone – held by the 5th Gordons, 4th Oxfords, and 8th Worcesters, fought with splendid gallantry throughout the day, and were still holding out at 4.10 p.m. when the buried cable – which had up to this hour remained intact – ceased to operate. The last message received was from Lieut. Cunningham, 4th Oxford and Bucks, who was then the senior Officer Commanding in Enghien Redoubt, asking permission for the garrison to try and cut their way out. This permission was given, and also, by Corps instructions, to the other Redoubts at the same time. Except for a few odd men that came in during the night, none returned from the battalions fighting in the Forward Zone.[6]

From *The Story of the 2/5th Gloucestershire Regiment 1914–18* (Crypt House Press, Gloucester).

MEMORANDA.

The Lewis Gun.

This gun is literally a machine-gun
but in practice is not so termed.
It is essentially an infantry weapon and is
supplementary to the Vickers Gun and the
rifle. Its chief advantages are that its

invulnerability, and mobility and chief
disadvantages its delicacy, the fact that
it is useless for setting up a barrage and
also that the system of air cooling employed
does not allow of more than 12 magazines being
fired continuously. The table below gives a
few facts and figures concerning the gun —

Weight	26 lbs.
" with mag. loaded	30½ "
No of cartridges in fully charged magazine	47 "

Action — by the gas of the discharged cartridge
Air cooled.
Supported by bipod in front and shoulder in rear.
Peephole backsight and blade foresight.
Cost — £175.
The rifling consists of 4 grooves running from
right to left

These notes were made by Arthur in 1918 during his training on the assembly and use of the Lewis gun.

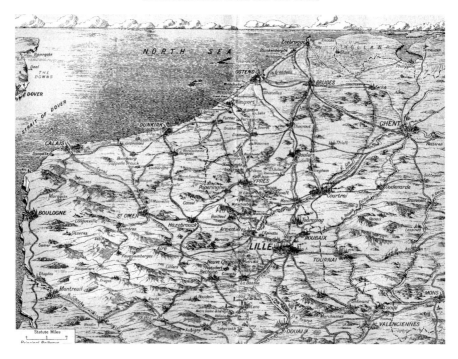

Map from a booklet belonging to Arthur, dating from around 1935, showing the area around Lille, including the villages of Armentières and Estaires, where he was in combat in 1918.

Before describing the remaining events of the day I must explain that I was No.1 of No.1 Platoon of 'A' Company, and as First Lewis Gunner I carried the gun, weighing about 35lb, and a revolver. The Second Gunner carried a bag containing spare parts, and the remaining five members of the team carried loaded pans of ammunition. All could fire the gun if required and all could effect repairs in seconds. Three quarters of the battalion which went into action that day were under twenty years of age, but they were highly trained – much better than the older soldiers – although of course the older soldiers had the fighting experience which we had not.

The objective of 'A' Company was a road about 500 yards away across a piece of completely open ploughed land. Along the road was a straggle of houses which might or which might not contain Germans. We had to cross it with no cover at all. There was no artillery on our side, but fortunately the German artillery fire was very desultory, presumably because, the front having disappeared, they did not know what to fire at. But I still didn't relish crossing that open space. However, it had to be done, and we did it in a series of rushes. I was very thankful to get under the cover of a brick wall. We cautiously explored the houses, but they were unoccupied. Then we came to a large farm built round a courtyard with two opposite gateways. Round each gateway were a heap of Portuguese dead and two or three Germans. We crossed a small river (the Clarence) and another (the Noe) and came to open country with houses about a quarter of a mile away. As it was getting into late afternoon we were ordered to dig in on the bank of the River Noe near Carvion Farm, by a small bridge which had some dead horses at the one end. In front of

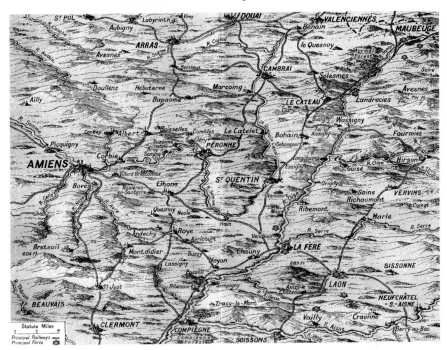

Map from the same booklet showing the area east of Amiens, in which Arthur saw action in
1918.

us was a British field gun which had been abandoned. While we were digging our post
we were fired at several times from the distant houses, but no one was hit. Surprisingly
nobody seemed bothered by the sniping – not even me. Perhaps it was because I could
not believe that on a nice sunny day anyone could be actually shooting to kill somebody.

Parallel to the two streams and just behind our post was the road from Robecq to
the village of Calonne. 'C' Company on our left took up position at Calonne after
driving out a few Germans.

Thus ended my first day in the line. I was just eighteen years and seven months old,
and I had chosen an auspicious day for my fighting debut because on 11 April Field
Marshal Sir Douglas Haig, Commander in Chief in France, issued a most dramatic and
famous Special Order of the Day to all ranks (see page 67). After briefly outlining the
critical situation, it ended with the ominous paragraph:

> There is no other course but to fight it out. Every position must be held to the last man:
> there must be no retirement. With our backs to the wall and believing in the justice of our
> cause each one of us must fight on to the end. The safety of our homes and the freedom of
> mankind alike depend upon the conduct of each one of us at this critical moment.

This must have been the turning point of the war, because from then on our division never gave an inch of ground and I believe that was true of every division in the
British Army.

The night was quiet except for the ever-present background rumble of the guns, and for a brief period of excitement when the sound of galloping houses was heard apparently charging right at us. But they stopped at the field gun, which they hitched up and galloped off.

It was our artillery, who to rescue the gun must have galloped right through the Germans and galloped back again.

The next day, Saturday 13 April, was to put our nearly raw battalion to the test. For the Germans launched a heavy attack on Calonne (held by 'C' Company). The road they used was at right angles to the Calonne/Robecq road and was about 400 yards to the left of our post. Hedges hid the attackers from us, except in one place where a large shell must have blown the hedges away and made a crater in the road. Men were streaming towards Calonne until we sighted the Lewis gun and all rifles on the gap and opened fire with everything we had got. There was instant confusion and Germans went in all directions. After that, groups would come at irregular intervals, dive into the shell crater for cover and then scramble out on the other side, but they were sitting ducks for us, and we fired the gun in turns till it was too hot to hold. It certainly relieved the heavy pressure on 'C' Company, who put up a splendid show and gave the Germans a real thrashing, although many of the young fellows who came from Norwich with me were killed or wounded.

During the engagement an officer of the Machine Gun Corps, who had been reconnoitring the line, dropped into our post and congratulated us on the effect our crossfire had had on the action. I must be excused for describing it in some detail, but it was a new experience and in fact we never again had the opportunity of using our gun with the same devastating effect. And, extraordinary to relate, during the whole affair not one shot was fired at our post.

One interesting aspect of the German breakthrough was that it brought the line into an inhabited area, and the departure of the people meant that the animals – cows, pigs and poultry – were left to look after themselves. The cows in particular suffered as they could not be milked. However, in our platoon we had a farm worker from Devon, so we rounded up the few cows nearest to us and he actually milked them in the front line! It was, of course, only a matter of time before they were all killed, so an order was issued from the battalion command that any fowls or animals brought in would be cooked by the battalion cooks and properly distributed.

Until the supply was exhausted, this provided a welcome addition to normal rations. Nor did we lack for wine. Nearly every house contained a supply, so this too was organised, one man from each post collecting wine in the water bottle at a set time, from houses properly allotted to each platoon.

After two or three days we were relieved and went back to billets in the cellars of the asylum at St Venant. Here, too, there was a fair amount of food left in the houses and shops, and the huge kitchens were filled all day with amateur cooks at their work. I did not relish going back into the line, but it had to be, and this in-and-out routine was to be ours for some time.

It was comforting to hear that our artillery was building up behind us and was playing an increasing part in the artillery strafing, which took place every two or three hours and which was most unpleasant while it lasted.

SPECIAL ORDER OF THE DAY
By FIELD-MARSHAL SIR DOUGLAS HAIG
K.T.. G.C.B.. G.C.V.O., K.C.I.E
Commander-in-Chief, British Armies in France.

To ALL RANKS OF THE BRITISH ARMY IN FRANCE AND FLANDERS.

Three weeks ago to-day the enemy began his terrific attacks against us on a fifty-mile front. His objects are to separate us from the French, to take the Channel Ports and destroy the British Army.

In spite of throwing already 106 Divisions into the battle and enduring the most reckless sacrifice of human life, he has as yet made little progress towards his goals.

We owe this to the determined fighting and self-sacrifice of our troops. Words fail me to express the admiration which I feel for the splendid resistance offered by all ranks of our Army under the most trying circumstances.

Many amongst us now are tired. To those I would say that Victory will belong to the side which holds out the longest. The French Army is moving rapidly and in great force to our support.

There is no other course open to us but to fight it out. Every position must be held to the last man: there must be no retirement. With our backs to the wall and believing in the justice of our cause each one of us must fight on to the end. The safety of our homes and the Freedom of mankind alike depend upon the conduct of each one of us at this critical moment.

D. Haig. F.M.

General Headquarters,
Thursday, April 11th, 1918.

Commander-in-Chief,
British Armies in France.

PRINTED IN FRANCE BY ARMY PRINTING AND STATIONERY SERVICES.   PRESS A—4/18.

This Special Order of the Day from Field Marshal Sir Douglas Haig was kept by Arthur and annotated with the following caption:

'This document must be one of the very few, if any, Orders of the Day once pasted onto the notice board of a battalion in the fighting line in France during the First World War.

Having regard to the size of the forces involved and the fact that the future of the world depended on the response to the appeal, this must be the most dramatic and fateful Order of the Day ever issued by a military commander in the history of warfare.'

The document encapsulates and emphasises the belief in heroic self-sacrifice for their country that was such an important motivating factor for the young men who served in the First World War.

OFFICIAL COPY.

[*Crown Copyright Reserved.*

FIELD ALMANAC

$$\frac{40}{\text{W.O.}}$$
4421

1918.

LONDON:
PUBLISHED BY HIS MAJESTY'S STATIONERY OFFICE,

To be purchased through any Bookseller or directly from
H.M. STATIONERY OFFICE at the following addresses:
IMPERIAL HOUSE, KINGSWAY, LONDON, W.C. 2, and 28, ABINGDON STREET, LONDON, S.W. 1;
37, PETER STREET, MANCHESTER; 1, ST. ANDREW'S CRESCENT, CARDIFF
23, FORTH STREET, EDINBURGH;
or from E. PONSONBY, LTD., 116, GRAFTON STREET, DUBLIN;
or from the Agencies in the British Colonies and Dependencies,
the United States of America and other Foreign Countries of
T. FISHER UNWIN, LTD., LONDON, W.C. 2

Price One Penny Net.

The title page of Arthur's 1918 Field Almanac, which was a pocket-sized factual handbook
issued to troops.

I have already referred to the extraordinary phlegm exhibited by British troops;
and a good example of this occurred a few days after we had dug in. Apparently there
was a salient which had to be straightened out. So one evening just before sunset
there was an artillery barrage on our right, the shells falling onto German positions
on our left. Then, under this barrage, a long extended line of soldiers could be seen
walking slowly forward at right angles to, and in front of, our line of posts. German
guns, machine guns and rifles opened up on them, but although a man dropped here
and there the line just came slowly on past our post and stopped about fifty yards
to the left of it. Except for a few Lewis gunners lying down and firing towards the

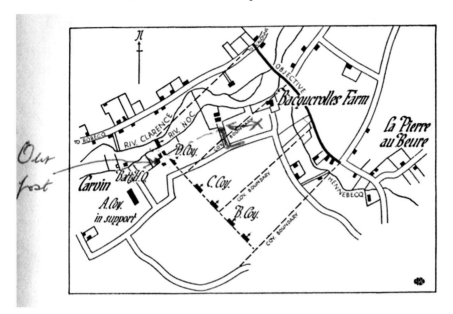

Map from page 117 of *The Story of the 2/5th Gloucestershire Regiment* by A.F. Barnes (Crypt House Press, Gloucester, 1930), annotated by Arthur. Page 114 describes how, on 13 April 1918, a German attack was repelled at a point between the villages of Calonne and Robecq by rifle fire from small isolated posts. Arthur has added, 'chiefly by my Lewis gun!' Beneath the map, he has written, 'From our post as shown above, the Lewis gun fired continuously into the flank of the German attack at X, causing casualties estimated at 400 by an independent officer of the Machine Gun Corps, and finally broke the attack.'

Germans, the rest, with spades and trenching tools, set about digging in, completely ignoring the German fire. Presently, when they had dug deep enough for protection, some of them actually leaned back against the parapet and lit up pipes and cigarettes. Meantime, out in the open under fire, the platoon stretcher-bearers – two to a platoon, and not protected by the Red Cross but only a white band round the left arm – bandaged the wounded and carried them back as quickly as they could. I watched in utter amazement and just could not believe that I was witnessing a real action, in which some of the men out there had just been killed and all were in danger of it. I do not know what division was engaged, but the men nearest to us belonged to the Hampshire Regiment. It was from this new line that the 2/5th Glosters made their attack on Bacquerolles Farm a few days later, and it can be seen in the map on page 117 of *The Story of the 2/5th Gloucestershire Regiment*.[7]

Until we were pulled out on 21 June for a rest at Molinghem, we were in and out of the line every three or four days, being relieved by the Glosters or the Berks, and there were only two personally exciting incidents to record during this period.

On 29 April my section, under a sergeant named Telling, was transferred to a post in 'No Man's Land' in advance of the British Line. Our job was to cover a particular German sniper and machine-gun post that was giving a lot of trouble. Only the sentry was allowed to look over the parapet during daylight and then in a different place each time. Early in the night we were visited by officers of a French mortar battery who were trying to locate the exact position of the German post, which they had orders to destroy. They went away, and most of us got down to sleep. Barnard and I were under some blankets at one end of the post. Suddenly there were explosions near the post, but the missiles came from behind! Then one landed right on the parapet just above Barnard and me and nearly sucked us out of the trench. Our French mortar people had mistaken us for the German post. It did not take us long to realise this and take shelter in some shell holes behind. Fortunately no one was injured, but the post was obliterated.

The other incident occurred when we were out of the line. We had just had lunch in a deserted farmhouse, with a few men in a room opposite, when a tremendous explosion took place at the front door. The room was filled with brick dust, which I found later had completely penetrated a half loaf of bread I had placed on a shelf behind my head and a piece of shrapnel had destroyed my canteen which contained the bread. A German shell had come through the front door and exploded in the passage. Miraculously no one was hurt. This farm was later to be the scene of perhaps the most frightening experience in my life.

From 21 June to 11 September I had a number of interesting experiences, but I lost the rough notes I made at the time and therefore cannot guarantee the chronological order.

I said we stayed a Molinghem, but I am sure that part of the rest was at a pleasant little hutted camp called Linghem, and here one night a ration of rum was issued. This was thick black Jamaican rum and was very strong. Many soldiers disliked it and did not drink it, but they drew their ration and gave it to one of the 'old sweats' who were always on the cadge. By this means, one old soldier (tattooed all over) had collected about a quart. This was almost a lethal dose if taken in one session, and many hut mates were apprehensive as to what would happen. He said he would be alright, but during the night I was awoken by a terrific row in the hut. Apparently our rum friend had got DT (delirium tremens). Quiet was restored by someone knocking him out. Blankets were thrown over him to keep him warm, and in the morning I was amazed to see the change in him. He went to bed plump and robust and got up like a mass of skin and bones. His blankets and the floor boards were saturated with sweat. So much for black Jamaican rum!

About this time I went to a Lewis gun refresher course at La Lacque. It was a pleasant little break of about a fortnight. My main impression was the effectiveness of Army training methods. As usual in any group there were some absolute dolts, but such was the repetition that everybody passed out 100 per cent efficient, the meaning of which will be appreciated when I say that part of the final test was to strip down the gun completely and then, blindfolded, put those 104 parts together again correctly in just one minute.

I was having so much trouble with my teeth that on 1 July, before breakfast, I hitchhiked by lorry to the 51st Casualty Clearing Station at Aire to see the dentist. This was a canvas hospital nearest to the line. The dental surgery was a bell tent, and I had to wait outside on a hot day until about 11 o'clock, watching men coming out spitting blood. When at last I went in, the dentist said he was going to take out twelve teeth, three top and three bottom at the back on each side. He injected cocaine, out came the teeth, and I left the tent, but what with the lack of food and excessive cocaine I was dizzy before I got to the camp entrance. I asked the chap on the gate to fetch somebody to see me, which he did while I sat on an upturned ration box. An RAMC orderly came and took me to a doctor who decided that my return to the battalion was out of the question. He explained that I should have to make the best of any accommodation, as the hospital was crowded out with men suffering from PUO (that great epidemic which swept the world and killed millions of people). At last my orderly found an empty stretcher for me in a marquee, and as I was bleeding profusely he got an empty fruit tin, quart size, from the refuse heap for me to spit into. I was thankful even for this, and there I lay spitting blood until the bleeding stopped late the next day and I was able to have a little food. By then the tin was nearly full.

The gods must have been on my side in that hospital, as you will understand when I tell you that my ward consisted of three large marquees end to end. The 'beds' were stretchers placed so close together that there was just standing room between them. They were arranged on each side and at right angles to a central fairway, so that there must have been hundreds of men in that ward, and everyone but me had PUO. Many died each day, but in spite of my very weak condition I did not catch it. And there are people who don't believe in miracles!

I must say something more about this PUO which may have medical and historical significance. Sometime in June our battalion came out of the line as usual to billets in cowsheds and other farm buildings. My platoon was in a cowshed, and we were sleeping on dry dung several feet thick (possibly the accumulation of centuries). When we went out to breakfast, several men complained of dizziness and fell down. They were found to have a high fever. The more I heard about the timing and progress of the epidemic the more I became convinced that this worldwide disease started that morning in that cowshed, from germs which had lain dormant there for a long, long time. When, therefore, I was later given *The Story of the 2/5th Gloucestershire Regiment* by my brother-in-law, Cyril Gibbs, it was with great interest that I read on page 124, 'It started with the Oxfords'.

I had to stay in the casualty clearing station until my mouth healed sufficiently to enable me to eat normal battalion rations, and during that time I did all sorts of fatigue jobs, including assisting with domestic chores for the officers' mess. While engaged on this job I slept with others in a canvas annexe to the mess marquee. It would take too long to report in detail all my experiences there, but I do remember with affection an American doctor of psychology who was a volunteer private in (I believe) the 91st Canadians, the Aberdeen journalist – also a private – who managed to write a seven-page letter to his wife every day although he went nowhere and did nothing but his jobs, the shell-struck cases who were so ably dealt with by a brilliant doctor named Watson (or Watkinson), and the infantry lieutenant who applied for permission to enter the hospital in a letter to the colonel which commenced 'Dear Sir, I have the honour to inform you I have contracted venereal disease'.

While I was in the casualty clearing station the practice of blood transfusion had its birth, and many desperate cases were treated. The patient lay on an operating table and the blood donor lay alongside him. The vein of the donor was cut on the front of the arm opposite the elbow and a tube connected this incision to the same place on the patient. It was too late for most of the patients, but in some cases they left substantial sums to the donors.

There was a call for volunteer donors, who would be well fed for four weeks before being asked to donate, and after donation they would convalesce for a week or two and then have three weeks' leave in England. This was too good a chance to be missed, so I volunteered. One of the doctors was a leading bacteriologist, and he tested the blood of the volunteers. Blood was divided into four classes, of which the only one of any real use was no.4, apparently because it would mix with any other blood. About one in three had no.4 blood. I was one of these. It meant I stayed in the hospital a week or two longer than I should have done, but I was not called upon to give blood, nor did I get the reward in leave.

I don't know why, but the team of volunteers was dispersed and I was sent back to the battalion. Unfortunately I did not know if the battalion was anywhere near where I left it on the Robecq front. Anyway, I hitchhiked on lorries back to Robecq and learnt that the battalion was in the line and would come out that night to billets, one of which was the farm whose door was blown in by a shell as I reported earlier.

There was no one in the farm, which had suffered more damage. There was nothing to do but wait till the battalion arrived at about 3.00 a.m. Darkness fell, which made it even more lonely. And then a German 'strafe' or artillery barrage started. (I should explain here that it was the custom of the Germans to regularly plaster with shells the roads behind the British front, and this was one of those strafes.) I knew it would gradually come along the road, with salvos landing in sequence at 100 or 200-yard intervals. Needless to say, I dived for cover, but the only cover were the half-ruined farm buildings adjacent to the road and separated from it by a thin brick wall. I got right down into a corner but knew it wasn't much use if there was a direct hit.

The salvos landed nearer and nearer until I estimated that the next one would land right on my barn. I was absolutely frantic with terror, largely because I felt that as no one knew I was there, I should vanish into thin air without anyone ever knowing what had happened to me. The salvo landed all right and blew away part of the barn, but it fell a few yards beyond, and I survived.

I can't remember exactly when, but I think it must have been out of the line on the Robecq front, that it was decided that it was time for the battalion to have a bath. It certainly was. The field cookers were brought up to a ruined farm to get water, and a motley array of tubs, galvanised tanks and so on was scattered about the surrounding fields. Bathing took place a company at a time, two men to a tub. Each had to fetch his own water in a petrol tin from the cookers, and put it in the tub.

It was a warm sunny day, and when the bathing was in full swing an observer could have been forgiven for thinking he was in the Elysian fields with about 200 naked men standing around in couples on the green grass. Unfortunately a German plane decided to fly over just then, and the pilot must have guessed what was going on, for within a minute or two, German shells started landing among the bathers, who, leaving clothes and everything else behind them, just fled for cover, leaping over hedges and ditches like gazelles. For the benefit of anyone interested in the question of the morale of the British troops, I can tell them that practically every man jack was shrieking with laughter. It was all so comic. No one was hit, and we all crept back in time and collected our belongings.

Towards the end of August we went up through Nieppe Forest in open trucks on a light railway and entrenched in the edge of the forest opposite Merville. Our stay there was possible because the Germans constantly lobbed poison gas shells (mustard, tear and phosgene) into the forest and it hung about like a fog under the trees, so that we had to wear gas masks continuously. It was most uncomfortable and nerve wracking.

Fortunately we did not stay there long as Marshal Foch's great offensive was under-way and the Germans were falling back. There was a series of day-to-day actions, which brought us, on about 11 September, to what had been the charming little town of Estaires. Alas it was now rubble. All the pumps and wells had been destroyed or poi-soned, except one in the main street, and the whole town had been ruined; our one night there was punctuated with explosions every few minutes. One did not know what was going up next. Was I glad to get out of there!

On 13 September we reached Sailly, where in a morning attack in swilling mud Corporal Wilcox (from Birmingham) won the VC for destroying four German machine-gun posts single-handed except for one assistant, who was awarded the Military Medal.

The Story of the 2/5th Gloucestershire Regiment provides an interesting background to what the 184th Brigade was doing during the month of September[8], and I would particularly refer the reader to the remark at the bottom of page 136, referring to Laventie[9]. I would also refer you to the map[10] which shows the old Laventie front and a distillery towards the right-hand side. These items are of particular interest to me for the following reasons.

In a series of local actions the Germans were driven back over the old Lavantie Front on to Aubers Ridge, a rise of land on the other side of which was the city of Lille. Following them past Armentieres (one of whose houses I touched with my hand, though I never walked down one of its streets), we came to the old breastworks at Lavantie which had been built in 1914. (Trenches could not be dug because of the high water table.) At the point where we looked over the breastworks the old German front was about a quarter of a mile away and the space in between was filled with masses of rusting barbed wire in great long rolls. No.1 Platoon of 'A' Company, which was my platoon of about forty men, was ordered to advance across this barbed wire in pursuit of the enemy. We found it very difficult, as the rolls were so big and unstable that one could not get on to the top of them. However, we found that once we did get on top of one of these masses we could actually walk along them. They were so thick, but if one fell off into one of the hollows help was needed to get up again. How we crossed that barbed wire I do not know, but, at the cost of torn uniforms, we did, and eventually found ourselves in front of the said distillery, which since 1914 had been turned into a concrete strong point. A few shots were fired at us, but whoever occupied it must have hurriedly left, so we cautiously occupied it and set sentries on the brick wall surrounding it.

We had no officer, only a sergeant in charge, nor had we any specific objective, and frankly having taken the distillery we did not know what else to do. From the top of the building we could see the old British breastworks marked by a line of white and splintered dead tree stumps, but there was no sign of any troops following us.

We lay about till well into the afternoon, being sniped at occasionally by Germans on Aubers Ridge. The sergeant then got really worried and asked for a volunteer to

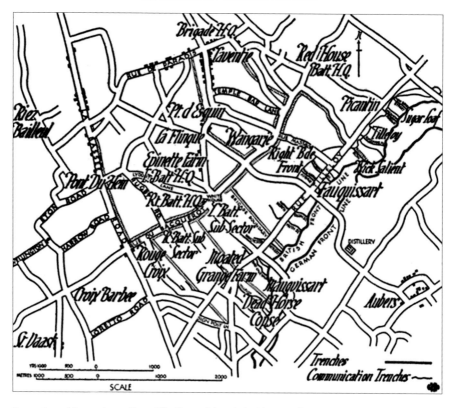

Laventie and its environs, from *The Story of the 2/5th Gloucestershire Regiment*, page 39.

go back to the old line and ask for instructions. I was fed up with doing nothing so offered to go, but when I got out on the barbed wire again I felt very lonely. It was impossible to keep a straight path and there were no distinguishing landmarks. I might as well have been on the moon. However, after a terrible journey I finally struck the breastworks. I soon found the company officer, Captain Jones, who said we had been ordered to halt on the old line as we were being relieved by a Grade 2 battalion of the Durham Light Infantry. He asked if I could take a relief in to the men in the distillery when the Durhams arrived, which would be after dark. I replied that it would be a tremendous job to take them in daylight and at night it would be impossible. He was very understanding and we decided to wait till the Durhams arrived. This they did at about 1 a.m. He gave them one look and decided they were incapable of getting there in daylight or dark.

Our battalion was being rapidly withdrawn, and only one company was left, so Captain Jones asked if I would go in again and bring the platoon out. I said I couldn't guarantee it in the dark, and that if I went alone the chances were ten to one I should get stuck all night on the wire. So he got two men to volunteer to go with me in case that happened.

We started off along the breastworks but hadn't gone far when I fell headlong into a deep shell hole full of water. I came out soaked. Obviously I could not go on, as the night was cold. Captain Jones agreed, told me to try and get some clothes from somewhere and left with the two men to try and catch up with the battalion.

I couldn't get any clothes from the Durhams so decided I too would try and catch the battalion. After a few minutes I struck a road crossing the front at right angles, and I made off along it as quickly as possible away from the front, but, alas, my luck was not in. The Germans knew that the British would be bringing up supplies on that road and they plastered it with shells continuously. I just had to get off it and take cover, which I did in an old dugout, and there I took off all my wet clothes, rubbed myself down as well as I could, then rubbed my body all over with rifle oil (i.e. whale oil) from a tin in my haversack as some protection against the cold. I had some difficulty in putting the wet clothes on again but managed finally and made off on a course parallel to but not on the road.

There was absolutely nobody or anything moving except me and the German shells, but at last I got away from them. I was feeling pretty tired, cold, miserable and completely lost when I came to an old German elephant hut and noticed a light coming under the door.

I went in and found one man – he was a signaller. I explained what had happened, but he said he couldn't help except with some bread, bully beef and tea, which were very welcome. He was concerned about my wet clothes, as there was no bed or blankets. However, I finally lay down on some wood chippings and went to sleep. Thus ended a day to be remembered.

I had a really good sleep and awoke refreshed but still wet. I resumed my journey and at last contacted other troops who could tell me where the battalion had gone. I caught up with them later in the day. Some hours later the men left at the distillery joined us. Apparently, as nobody contacted them they decided to withdraw and had a devil of a job getting out. It was four or five days before my clothes dried out on me, and I wore them all the time, awake and asleep. I didn't even catch a cold – a fact I attribute to the whale oil.

During the advance to the Lavantie Front an event took place which calls for some comment. I refer to the capture of a German strong point, Junction Post, by the Glosters. This is dealt with fairly fully in the pages of their book, to which I have referred. But the record as given does not correspond with my own recollections.

It is true that the Glosters captured the post, and they were so exhausted that no one could come back for rations, so we took them up on a night so wet that the water swished about inside my tunic above the belt, and around my knees above the putties! We, the Oxfords, took over Junction Post from the Glosters, and I clearly remember walking round and finding the bodies of two officers whose records I took out of their pockets. One was Captain Eric Harvey and the other was Lieutenant Jackson. Harvey was dressed in that fine greenish khaki commonly worn by officers, but Jackson's uniform was comparatively new and his tunic was of that inferior cloth (a kind of a brownish serge) often worn by officers promoted from the ranks and not very well off.

From the papers on Harvey's body I was startled to learn that this was the Eric Harvey of Minsterworth, whose kick in the groin of my brother-in-law, Harry Hall, led to his premature death. I am not blaming Harvey for this. It was just an accident. But what a coincidence!

These two modest medals were the acknowledgement that Arthur received (in common with all private foot solders) for his service in the First World War. They were subsequently worn by him once a year, on Remembrance Day. Upper image: obverse; lower image: reverse.

Five

'The Byng Boys Were Here'

Pack up your troubles in your old kit bag
And smile, smile, smile.
While you've a lucifer to light your fag,
Smile, boys, that's the style.
What's the use of worrying?
It never was worthwhile!

(First World War song)

At the beginning of October the 61st Division was moved to a totally different part of the front, near Cambrai. Exactly how we got there I can't remember, but one or two snapshots still remain with me: the division on the march filling the road as far as one could see – quite a thrilling sight; myself and one other man as liaison men out in front of the battalion marching through Doullens; a terrible train journey ending during the night at (I believe) Havrincourt; a night march on and on, apparently to nowhere, until at last we were led off the road onto some open grassy waste and told to get what sleep we could, how we could, with no cover at all – not even overcoats. But what a sight awaited us in the morning – a sight which was afterwards recorded in Nelson's *History of the Great War*, clearly from observation at that very spot.

Our nearest horizon was about 300 yards away, and it was obviously a great arterial road, for the whole horizon was filled for miles in each direction with marching men silhouetted against the sky. It was, in fact, the great straight road from Bapaume to Cambrai, and it sloped slightly downwards each way from where we were.

I must explain that Cambrai and Douai were the bastions of the Hindenburg Line and were regarded as impregnable. The First Battle of Cambrai – where tanks were used for the first time on any scale – had just failed, mainly due to lack of reserves. So when General Byng was given the task of taking it in 1918 he made sure he had all the troops and supplies he wanted to sustain the attack day and night until the Germans were broken, and it was the tail end of this tremendous battle that we were about to witness – the sort of war panorama which comparatively few people on the ground could ever expect to see.

It wasn't long before most of our battalion assembled along the side of the road. Cambrai had already been taken, and the front had moved to a ridge beyond. A line of captive balloons marked the line of the front, and occasionally one of these went

As Arthur explains in his account, little remained to show that Bourlon Wood had actually ever been a wood at all, after fierce fighting had taken place there during the First Battle of Cambrai.

up in flames, having been hit by a shell or a German aeroplane. Watching carefully, one could see the movement of what looked like black shadows. Those shadows were masses of troops being deployed and withdrawn to a strict timetable. The battlefield was being fed by our road. One endless column of troops was marching in, and on the same road another endless column was marching out, while alongside the road a light railway was carrying up shells and supplies.

But what made the heart beat faster was the sound of music – the battalions were marching in with bands playing, and these bands were playing out the tired troops who were being relieved. Over half a million men could be seen from one position. It was a spectacle on a grand scale, of irresistible military might operated on a clock-work basis with an assurance and buoyancy of spirit which baffles description.

We spent the day on the scrounge. To the west of Cambrai a huge area which had been fought over again and again was just a waste of weeds and rubble. The sites of villages could just be distinguished by grey smudges caused by the powder into which they had been pulverised, and here and there among the weeds and rubble were helmets, rifles, wrecked tanks, and shattered guns. One humorist had chalked on the side of a wrecked German gun 'The Byng Boys were here'. We spent the night in bivouacs and dugouts in Bourlon Wood – the scene of fierce fighting in the First Battle of Cambrai. It wasn't much like a wood, more like a lot of crooked matchsticks stuck in the ground.

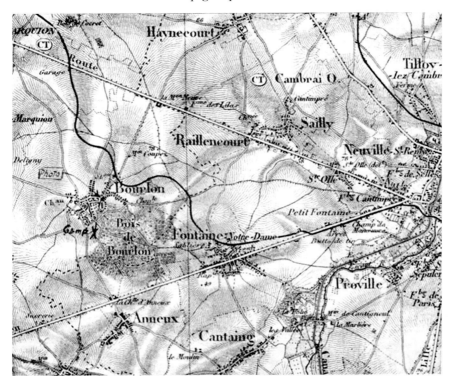

A map fragment on which Arthur marked his company's camp just outside Bourbon Wood and also the location of where the photograph on page 78 was taken.

A few days later we marched through the empty echoing streets of Cambrai, with the band playing, and reached the village of Cagnoncles. We arrived about 19 October and stayed for about five days, during which we gave half our rations to the near-starving populace. The division was in Corps Reserve, and on about 24 October we spent the night lying on the brick floor of a house in St Aubert. The Germans must have made a stand, for we were warned that there would be a big artillery bombardment in the morning. About 5 a.m. it was opened by the firing of a big gun. Then it started.

We were some 5km behind the front, but the concussion was so enormous that our floor quivered. At about 11 a.m. we were ordered into Division Reserve and then into Brigade Reserve, which meant we marched up through the lines of artillery: 12ft and 9ft long-range guns, then the 6ft naval guns and later the 4ft 5in and field guns, but my memory is of a line of 6ft batteries. The teams were stripped to the waist and working like demons loading the guns. As we passed, one battery ceased firing while teams of horses charged to them at the gallop. They were hitched up, and the horses tore up the road with them. We passed them farther on, and they had taken up position again and were firing like mad while teams of horses galloped back for other guns. Meantime, observation balloons with their cables attached to lorries were being moved slowly up one by one as the Germans were driven back. A smallish hill on our left seemed to be a point of resistance on which the guns were concentrating. It pro-

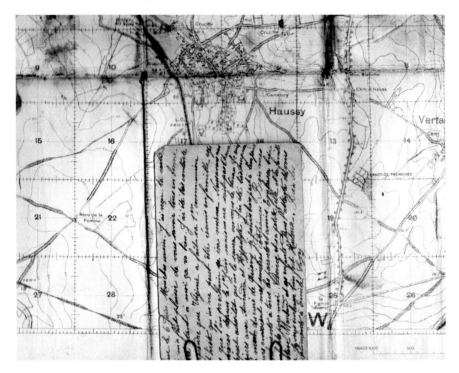

Haussy, on a detail of the large map alluded to in the text, which Arthur was lucky enough to obtain. Attached is the postcard found by Arthur on the school floor. Apparently oblivious of the war, the writer (Emile) refers to family matters including 'Virginie's first communion'.

vided an amazing sight, for the shells were falling so thick and at such speed that the flash of their bursting seemed to cover the hill with a sheet of fire. It was incredible that anything could survive there. I am bound to confess that the sight gave me great satisfaction. The Germans asked for war and they were getting it.

Actually we did not go into action on this occasion, nor even right into the line. On the 23rd we passed through Haussy[11] on the way to Bermerain, and I particularly remember Haussy for several reasons: because I picked up an interesting postcard in the schoolroom where I spent the night; because I saw several people who had been mutilated by the Germans (one with both hands cut off); because I saw the spot where several leading citizens had been rounded up by the Germans and shot; and because we again surrendered part of our rations to help the desperate food situation.

It must have been the evening of the 24th when we arrived at the small town of Bermerain, because we acted as reserves to the Glosters who that night attacked Vendegies-sur-Ecaillon just north-west of Bermerain. Details of their night attack are given in *The Story of the 2/5th Glosters*. It is remarked there that 'maps were scarce'. I mention it because among my treasured souvenirs is one of those scarce maps, which was actually used to direct the battle and still has on it some of the Vendegies mud!

But that map is precious to me for another and much more personal reason. About 27 October we marched out of Bermerain and deployed along the bottom of a shal-

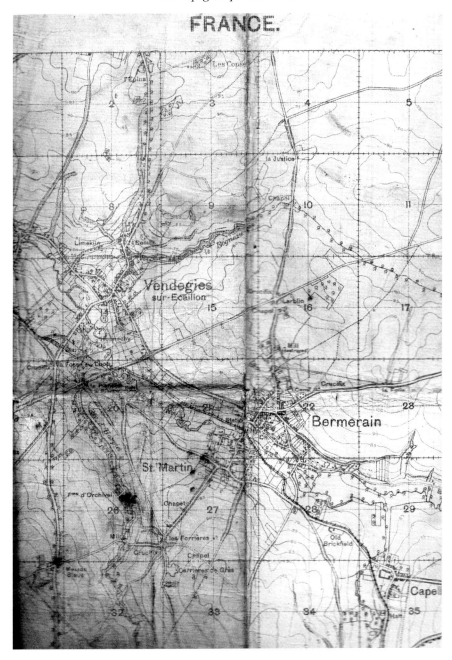

A detail of the large map alluded to in the text, showing the area around Vendegies and Bermerain. Arthur notes that it was one of only six copies in circulation and still bears vestiges of mud from the battlefield.

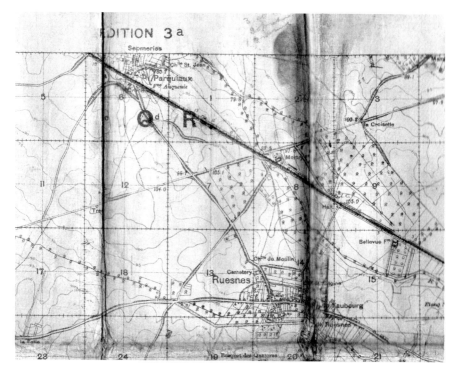

Detail of the map mentioned in the text, showing the village of Sepmeries at the top; the wood (square 9R) where the German guns were; and the trenches (Q12, on the crease in the map) where Arthur and his fellow infantrymen were nearly obliterated.

low valley to the north-east. The actual line is shown in section Q of the map by a line of trees (actually some odd bushes) crossing squares 17 and 18. Here we relieved some Northumberland Fusiliers. Apparently the actual position of the Germans was unknown, so we remained for some hours while reconnoitring took place. At last we were ordered forward, to keep going till contact was re-made. So we started off up a slope to the north-east, in the direction of Sepmeries. We were in extended formation, but as we ascended the slope barbed wire, which sloped inwards to a gap on the crest, caused everybody to naturally converge. So a rather jumbled up body of men passed through the gap. As we were doing so, German shells landed all round, apparently fired point-blank from guns among the trees in square 9 of section R. In front of us were some German practice trenches, shown on the left side of square 12Q, and everybody jumped into them for cover. These trenches were then plastered with 5ft 9in shells. I realised what was happening, and although it is dangerous to get out of a trench during a bombardment I decided it was less dangerous than staying and almost certainly being killed, so I scrambled out and started to run down the slope towards the sunken road in square 8Q. The crew of one of the German guns must have decided to have a bit of sport with me, for I hadn't gone many yards when I heard a shell coming straight at me. By the time it reached me I was on the ground, and it exploded a few yards beyond. I got up and ran again, and again a shell came straight at me, unquestionably aimed at me personally as there was nothing else to aim at. But, of course, I was on the ground when it burst. This was repeated two or three times more, by which time I had reached the shelter of trees and banks in the valley. I was panting with fright and lack of breath, but I soon recovered. I was surprised to find the position occupied by other British troops who were resting for a while. They had witnessed the episode I have described, and I had a lot of sympathy, though I was strictly not following 'the books'. Eventually everybody did what I did, but I regret to say that, because they did not do it quickly enough, many casualties had been sustained, including the deaths of two men who had come nearly all the way through the war, to within about fourteen days of the Armistice.

Between 26 October and 1 November we seemed to shuttle backwards and forwards between Bermerain and Maresches. I can't remember which time we were in which place, but I do remember quite vividly certain incidents.

There was the afternoon when another division passing through temporarily stopped in Bermerain and the streets were packed with men of both divisions, hopelessly mixed up. A number of NCOs of our battalion pushed their way through the milling crowd shouting for all men of the Oxfords to get out onto open ground north of the village. There we were formed up into companies, and officers explained that we had been pulled out on orders from Colonel Flanagan in case a German aeroplane reported the mass of troops in the village as a wonderful target for the German artillery. How right he was.

Although there was no shelling at the time, we were split up into small sections of about eight men per section. Each section took up position some yards from the other, so that we covered a large area. Instructions were given that on a whistle signal each section would kneel down facing north with everyone pressing close to one another. It was late afternoon when the first shells came over, and they kept coming over for four or five hours. Most landed in the village, but many landed among our knots of kneeling men. Much damage and many casualties were caused in Bermerain, but not one man of the Oxfords was injured. Colonel Flanagan was strongly commended in despatches for his foresight and action.

On another night we were in reserve to troops attacking Maresches. Our platoon was killing time in some village, which I think must have been Sepmeries, when about 1 a.m. the platoon commander, Lieutenant Passmore (a very popular officer), came along to say that the troops in the line at the top of a ridge were short of small-arms ammunition and we were to take it up to them. Boxes of ammunition had been dumped in the road by horse transport which apparently could get no further. These boxes were very heavy and had rope handles at the ends. There were fourteen of us and six boxes, so two men were allotted to each box and the two men over were to act as relief. But obviously two men could not act as relief to twelve. We started off but did not get far before a rest was necessary, and these rests became necessary at shorter and shorter intervals. Presently somebody said to Passmore that it was impossible for us to carry six boxes and some would have to be dumped. Passmore said 'No', whereupon one pair put down their box and the rest followed suit. After a minute or two Passmore ordered us to pick them up and proceed, but no one moved. He then took out his revolver and said he would give the order again and shoot anyone who

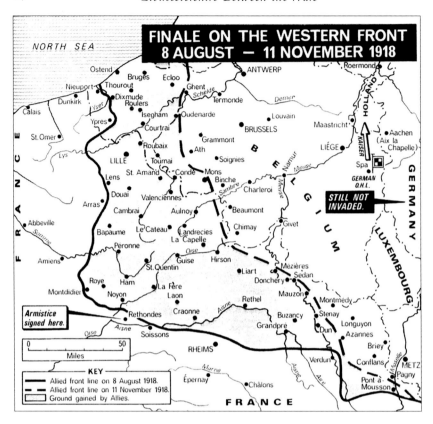

A map by Arthur Banks (1973) from *A Military Atlas of the First World War* (Pen and Sword Books) showing the area and events referred to in this chapter.

disobeyed. Instead of obeying, several men put a cartridge into the breech of their rifles, and somebody told Passmore if he didn't put his revolver away and stop talking nonsense he would shoot him then and there. I can't remember all that took place, but somehow it was made clear to Passmore that they had nothing against him personally, that he was in no position to dictate to us, that there was no mutiny but it was literally impossible to do what was asked. Finally, after a very exhausting journey, we managed to get three boxes to the top of the ridge.

The Germans were finally cleared out of Maresches on 1 November. That night was passed by 'A' and 'C' companies lying on a bank just east of Maresches. I believe there was a road on the top of it, but there was certainly a cabbage field beyond. An attack was to be launched at dawn on an eleven-mile front. We, of course, did not know this at the time, but it was the start of the Battle of Valenciennes, in which seven British divisions attacked eleven German divisions. Just before dawn all hell was let loose, and over the top we went, behind a creeping barrage which passed just over our heads and burst forwards a short distance ahead. This barrage lifted at the end of each minute and it was necessary to adjust the pace forward to avoid walking into it. Two companies of the 2/5th Glosters were advancing in extended formation on our right and they did just that, with the result that they sustained casualties and had to withdraw in confusion and reform.

I had been 'over the top' on three occasions before but only in limited actions. This was a real battle with a tremendous artillery bombardment. The noise was terrific and the only thing that could be heard above the shells, which were bursting everywhere, was the crackling of the Vickers machine guns. Even if you shouted at the top of your voice you couldn't hear yourself, and all orders were given by hand signals.

Our first objective was a road with a few scattered houses, about three quarters of a mile from our starting point. As we got near it the Germans blazed away with everything they had got. So while one section moved forward another covered them from shell holes and the like. I had the Lewis gun and the gun team stayed with me.

While temporarily sheltering in a very deep shell hole someone called attention to an action about thirty yards away. Looking across I saw Corporal Wilcox (whose VC had not then come through) walking towards a German machine-gun post, firing from the hip so that his bayonet was ready for use instantaneously. He had apparently outflanked the field of fire of the Nordernfelt gun and the Germans were coming out with their hands up. Wilcox still advanced in a manner so menacing that one young German (presumably reasoning that if death was certain he might as well take his attacker with him) leapt back into the post, wrenched the machine gun off its seating and fired straight at Wilcox (we afterwards learned he was wounded in one leg), who flung himself into the post and bayoneted the German. The other Germans stood stunned until Wilcox crawled out again, and holding his rifle in one hand he detached his ground sheet with the other. He then lay on it, covering the Germans all the time, and pointed to the four corners. They got the message, picked up the ground sheet (and Wilcox) and proceeded to the British lines. All this could hardly have taken more than a minute. The speed of thought and action were amazing – to say nothing of the ferocity –and yet normally Wilcox was one of the mildest of men.

We had hardly finished with Wilcox before one of the other men called attention to happenings on the left where, at the bottom of a slope, a large body of German soldiers marching in fours in an orderly manner were heading for the British front. I thought we were being outflanked and was about to open up on them with the Lewis gun, when at the end of the column I spotted a diminutive Tommy with his rifle slung on his shoulder and I realised they were prisoners and he was the guard taking them back – one hundred were taken.

We reached our objective without much difficulty or delay, and were given another about a mile further on. This, too, was reached quickly and orders were given to dig in for the night and prepare for a counter-attack. Darkness fell and a message came that we being relieved as another division was coming through. This meant that the relieving troops would have to be brought in and guided to their positions. I hated standing about doing nothing, so I volunteered for the job (as I did frequently). I walked along the line to see where everybody was and strolled back to find Company or Battalion HQ.

Our line was east of two timber plantations divided by an open avenue which would form a natural passage through, and as I walked back I was intrigued by a light shining out through an open door. When I got to it I found the light came from a bulb inside a British tank which had been converted by the Germans and used against us. I had hardly got there when German shells started to fall in the vicinity so I smashed the bulb and got away as quickly as possible. It was all a bit eerie and mysterious but I decided that the light was left on deliberately to give the German gunners a ranging mark in the dark.

I found Company HQ, collected the relief, took them in to their allotted positions and as I did so our men collected and formed up to retire. The time may have been about 2 a.m. You can imagine that by now we were all more than a bit tired and hungry but we had a long way to go yet – all the way back to Bermerain. We started off alright but the night was still and damp – just right for gas, and the Germans knew it. They fired over hundreds of gas shells which formed a white mist difficult to see through without a gas mask, but the mist was poison gas, which meant we all had to wear gas masks. Someone who has not experienced it can only imagine what it is like to find one's way through a fog at night wearing a gas mask partly filled with saliva.

We just blundered on until we came to a barbed wire entanglement. Somehow or other, though we were virtually blind, this was surmounted by everybody except me, and I was handicapped by carrying a Lewis gun weighing nearly 40lb. Nobody could see anybody and we could only keep together by making a noise. As I struggled to get out of the wire I could hear the voices receding, although I shouted, and I began to panic. I just had to take the risk of momentarily taking off my mask, and saw that I had been going along the entanglement instead of across it. I was soon clear and chasing after the distant voices. I caught them before they got to the bank from which our attack was originally launched, and here I was again to witness the behaviour of men in a state of complete and utter exhaustion.

Fortunately, we were out of the gas area and masks had been removed, but when we came to the tip of the deep and steep bank below the road we had started from in the morning, the men were so exhausted they could not be bothered to climb down properly. They just let themselves go and pitched head over heels down the bank in the darkness and landed in a heap at the bottom.

We scrambled over a small stream into a wet ploughed field which was planted with turnips or kohlrabi. Not only was everybody tired but ravenously hungry and the gas had made us thirsty too. Everybody just sat down in the mud, tore the turnips out of the ground, wiped the mud off roughly and ate them raw. Eventually we got to our feet and moved on – just a rabble. Then we came across a stack of petrol tins filled with brook water, which had been provided for cooling the guns. Whoever could, grabbed one and staggered on, stopping every now and then for a gulp from his precious tin. How many times we fell on our faces in the mud I do not know, but eventually we reached a road not far from Bermerain, which we entered singing! Would you believe it?

Alas I have to record that on this trek back to Bermerain one of the company's Lewis gunners was so fed up with carrying the gun that when crossing a bridge outside the town he flung the gun over the parapet. There was an awful rumpus about this, but it was nothing to another rumpus which took place the next day.

I must explain that the news of our going into action was known to everybody in the battalion, so members of the band and other non-combatants approached us

to bring back souvenirs in the form of automatic pistols or binoculars. I had promised to secure a pistol for one of the bandsmen. In the course of the action I had
secured three automatic pistols – one long-barrelled Luger and two beautiful small
ones. I regret that when I was rifling packs left in a German post I found a lovely pair
of Geiss binoculars which I placed on the parade of the post while I continued my
search. I had hardly done so when one of a group of soldiers passing the post stooped
down and purloined my find. However, I still had the three pistols, and when we had
cleaned up on the morning after our return to Bermerain, the cooks, bandsmen and
so on crowded round for souvenirs. I duly delivered the one I was asked to get, and
sold this and the other small one for ten francs each. I was going to keep the Luger,
but the big-drummer in the band offered me twenty francs for it, and as I thought
I could get another for myself next time I sold it to him. He had no idea how to use it
and nearly shot me with it, so I extracted the magazine, explained the safety catch and
warned him never to point it at anyone.

You can imagine my feelings when, just after the midday meal, messengers came
round to say the colonel had ordered all pistols to be handed in to Battalion HQ
immediately. Enquiring the reason for the order we learnt that the big-drummer had
shot himself through the stomach and a fellow bandsman through the foot. I believe
he died in hospital. I was very alarmed as I thought that in the ensuing inquiry
I should be in trouble, but my alarm proved to be unnecessary.

After a brief rest in Bermerain we marched back to Maresches.

Six

Armistice

Now are our brows bound with victorious wreaths,
Our bruised arms hung up for monuments,
Our stern alarums turned to merry meetings,
Our dreadful marches to delightful measures.
Grim-visaged War hath smoothed his wrinkled front.

(William Shakespeare, *Richard III*)

It must have been about 7 November. Supplies had come up for the battalion canteen, and I had been commissioned by some of my pals to stand in the queue and collect whatever chocolate, tins of fruit, evaporated milk and cigarettes were obtainable. (Perhaps I should explain that supplies of these items were limited, so whoever got in the front of the queue was supposed to purchase what he could for his pals before the supply was exhausted and only inferior cigarettes, 'soldiers' friend', and boot polish were left.)

Meantime my own dinner was being kept warm for me in the billet. I heard my Christian name called, and there was my brother Wallace who had been brought along by someone in the billet. He was in the band of the Shropshire Light Infantry who were trying to catch up with their battalion. They had been marching for days with hardly any food, so I bought some extras from the canteen and took him to the billet with some of his pals, and I persuaded our battalion cooks to provide them with dinner. After this we went to the ruined house his band was resting in, where he tried to persuade them to refuse to proceed until they had some proper food. But it was no use, and at about 3 p.m. off they marched and that was that.

Then we heard that we had a new Brigadier General – Carton de Wiart. Cold shivers went down the back of everyone in the brigade, for he had an unsurpassed record as a fire-eater, missing no chance of throwing the men under his command into whatever fighting happened to be going. The battalion was paraded for his inspection on the flat above Maresches to the east. We looked very much the worse for wear, with patched and dirty uniforms. I had no buttons on my trousers, which were held by nails through the braces, and the leather laces on my boots were broken, one having a knot on the outside.

General de Wiart arrived, and I was very interested to see this legendary hero whose medals included the VC and the highest honours for bravery that many countries

This card with its message of 'Good Luck' actually contained a Christmas greeting from Arthur to his family.

could award. I was not disappointed. He arrived on a lively cob with his cap tilted at a rakish angle, and a shade over the place where one of his eyes had been. He got down unaided from his horse although he had only the stump of one arm and, I believe, an artificial leg. I noticed also that he had eleven wound stripes, two for the Boer War and nine for the First World War!

Colonel Flanagan called the battalion to attention and handed over to de Wiart, who promptly ordered 'Stand at ease. Stand easy'. He then said, 'Just come to attention individually as I come to you', and the first man he came to was me, for I was first in the front rank. I came to attention. He looked me all over and passed on without comment till he got to about the fourth along when, to my utter astonishment, he looked back at me and said 'Get that bootlace changed'. Not bad for a chap with one eye! Thank goodness the war ended before we had to go into action again.

Rumours that the end might come quickly were circulating on 10 November, and then, on the morning of 11 November, our platoon paraded in a lane outside our billet. It was bitterly cold and the road was covered in frozen snow and ice. The officer in charge said he had to read an order of the day, which he proceeded to do. It commenced, 'Hostilities will cease at 11.00 this morning'.

The reaction of his listeners astounded me. This was the announcement which they had all longed for years to hear. It was the best news they could possibly hope for. The announcement was received in dead silence and without any reaction at all.

The parade was dismissed, and we had a few hours off before doing fatigue work in the afternoon to repair a railway line damaged by the retreating Germans. The afternoon also saw the return of many of the French residents of Maresches, who quarrelled over possession of such furniture as remained, and who would have torn the beds from under the British soldiers if they had not been stopped and forcibly cleared out till we left.

Within a few days we were back at Cambrai and billeted in the citadel, which consisted of barracks built on top of a walled mound. The most striking thing about this place was the name that the Germans had gven it – General von Wetter Kaserne – painted in enormous letters on the outside retaining wall[12].

During the short time we were there we had the opportunity of seeing the battalions of the famous 51st Highland Division (who had been specially issued with new uniforms) drilling for their unique march to Cologne to form part of the Army of Occupation. It was all very impressive.

The day came to entrain for camps nearer the Channel. We marched on to Cambrai station and waited for the train to come in, but it did not come because a message had been received that the station had been mined and might go up at any minute. We were hurriedly marched back to barracks and German prisoners were brought in to dig out the mines. It was three days before they were cleared and we departed – fifty to a truck as usual.

The train stopped in the middle of a very wet night in open country and we tumbled out and formed up in some sodden fields, where our field kitchens (which had gone on ahead three days before) were awaiting us with hot bully-beef stew. Unfortunately it contained a lot of onions and in the three days it had been prepared (waiting for us) these had gone sour – so much so that although the men were very hungry they simply could not eat it. I mention this because it was on this occasion that I performed one of my greatest gastronomic feats, for I actually consumed about three pints of this awful stew. I may add that all the time I was in the Army I was hungry, and all my pay went on biscuits, tinned milk, chocolate and cigarettes.

We had detrained at the nearest spot on the railway to our destination, the large village of Domart-en-Ponthieu. This was a very pleasant village in a pretty valley. Our stay here was enjoyable in spite of the fact that it was winter. Mornings were spent drilling and afternoons at organised sport – football, for example. It is traditional in the Army that the officers wait on the men at Christmas dinner, and Christmas 1918 was no exception. It was held in the upper floor of the Market House, and at the end of the dinner Colonel Flanagan made a speech which proved to be somewhat sentimental. I may have mentioned that he was a bachelor and a highly esteemed regular officer, dedicated to the Army. He had been put in command of a territorial battalion as part of his punishment for (we understood) striking a senior officer at a war conference. After some chat about Christmas and how time would be filled in till demobilisation he wound up by saying, 'When I was appointed to command this territorial battalion I hated the very sight of you, and I think you hated the sight of me too. But we have been through some difficult times together and you have always done what was asked of you so that', and he really did say this, 'I have learned to love you'. And he burst into tears.

While at Domart we had a battalion cross-country race over about seven miles. The whole battalion participated and I am pleased to say I won it. The prize was a folding writing case and two days' leave in Abbeville. I can't remember what happened to the writing case but I enjoyed the days in Abbeville.

Our brigade was billeted in three adjacent villages, of which ours, Domart, was by far the best. The other two, where the Glosters and Berks were billeted, were very poor[13]. With the men having nothing much to do and anxious for demobilisation, the morale of both battalions deteriorated to a point where the Glosters mutinied and physically attacked the colonel and adjutant. There were also acts of indiscipline by the Berks. Colonel Flanagan wasn't having any of that, so a general battalion parade was ordered to take place on one of the hills above Domart and every man in the battalion had to be present – transport, band, cooks and sundries. There he sat on his horse and addressed us in the following terms:

> This is the first time I have seen the whole battalion on parade at one time, and I welcome all the strange new faces. Where have you been hiding yourselves? The reason you are here is for me to inform you that there has been mutiny in the Glosters and trouble among the Berks. I am not going to have any mutiny in the Oxfords. I understand you all want to get home now the war has ended, but rioting will not hasten matters. You have just got to be patient and reasonable. If, however, any man has a genuine complaint I invite him to stand out here now and make it, but it had better not be trivial. It may be that we shall be called upon to suppress the mutiny among the Glosters and Berks, and if so it will be suppressed.[14]

I am pleased to say our services were not required for such a disagreeable task, and our stay in Domart was like a holiday. A barn in the village was converted into a theatre, and a brigade magazine called *Sircle Snips* was published (I have a copy of the first – and last – issue).

Reference to the theatre reminds me of an experience I would not have missed for worlds. Due to restlessness among troops waiting for demob, the authorities arranged some lectures to prepare us for the great day. I was detailed to attend one of these on the subject of demobilisation itself. As I have said, the theatre was a converted barn and the lighting in the afternoon was somewhat dim, so that I could not see the lecturer in any great detail, though I could distinguish that he was an officer. Describing the routine procedure to be followed, he moved from end to end of the stage, going through the motions and making a racy commentary (mixed up with a lot of swearing) while doing so. This somewhat unusual address made me sit up and take notice. I was amazed to see (as the speaker came under the light from a skylight at one end of the stage) that he was an Army chaplain. I was even more amazed when his talk proceeded from business routine to his experiences as an authority on Army morale, to army morals and how the troops should behave themselves while waiting to go home. It was the most extraordinary talk I have ever heard. The theatre was packed with men from all battalions in the brigade. They were not long out of the line and they were a very rough, tough lot, but they sat there spellbound. I had heard of preachers who could make people laugh or cry at will, but I had never believed it till now – for that is just what he did. When I saw Private Hustler in tears I knew I had seen every-thing. And what a climax. Having dealt with his subject, he said:

> Many of you listening to me may have been concerned and upset at my use of swearing and coarse language. I am not proud of it, but my object is to get your attention and interest. To do this I resort to the device of speaking to you in the language you use to one another. However, you know I have achieved my object, and if I have sinned in the methods I have used I shall be forgiven by Jesus Christ whom I am proud to serve.

At which everybody sprang to their feet and cheered him to the echo. On get-ting outside I enquired, 'Who on earth was that?' 'That was the Reverend Studdert Kennedy —"Woodbine Willie"', I was told. What a man!

Alas all good things come to an end, and so did our stay in Domart. The battalion entrained for Etaples, except the transport, consisting of cookers, GS wagons and limbers, all drawn by horses and mules. I was one of those detailed to accompany the column on foot, my job being to apply brakes on one of the limbers when going downhill and release them when going uphill. The driver could not do this as the limber consisted of two boxes hinged in the middle. To do my job I had to walk behind the limber ready for immediate action, but it meant that the mules of the next vehicle were breathing down my neck, and I did not like it very much.

When we started on our journey of 84km (about 52 miles) the roads were covered with frozen snow and ice, and it was terribly cold, so you can imagine that as the column only travelled at walking pace the riders of the horses and mules were nearly frozen in their saddles. Although I had to walk, it had the advantage of keeping me warm. Not far from the village of St Riquier the rider on the mules behind me asked if I would change places with him so that he could get some circulation into his body. I didn't like the idea at all because although I was sorry for him I had never been on a mule before and this was a pair of black Spanish mules with a reputation for being terribly hard to control. I explained this to him, but he was in such a state that at last I agreed, and mounted. He warned that I must maintain a very tight rein and under no circumstances must I let them get out of the column.

I endeavoured to do what he told me, but it was hopeless. Those mules knew immediately that I was no horseman and they decided they were going to have some fun. They edged to the left and I pulled on the right reins. They still edged and I still pulled, until I had their necks so bent they were nearly looking back at me. At last they edged out and, with a clear road in front, they bolted. The road was covered with a sheet of ice, but that didn't bother them. They flew past the front of the column down a steep hill to a bridge over a stream, then up the hill on the other side, but they kept slipping on the ice, and some riders who had chased us caught up with us. 'Don't get off', they shouted, and I tried to stay on, but by now the mules were frantic and kept slipping down on their knees. I was as frightened as they were frantic, so when my mule went down on its knees next time I gently slid over his head onto terra firma. So ended the greatest feat of horsemanship I have ever performed.

It took us two and a half days to get to Etaples, which meant that we had to spend two nights in two small villages, which were really clusters of farm buildings and cottages, mostly built of wattle and daub. The first night I had to sleep on the floor of the schoolroom near the door, where there was a very cold draught. When I got up in the morning I could hardly stand and knew I was running a high temperature. No medical attention was available and we had to go on, so I got the estaminet owner (next door) to give me some boiling black coffee with lashings of cognac and, well muffled up in my great coat, I hung onto the back of the limber for support. It wasn't long before I was drenched in sweat. By the end of the day my clothes had dried on me and I was as right as rain.

About the middle of the third day we arrived in Etaples – the great infantry transit camp I had heard so much about. It was covered with snow, and dotted all over the landscape were small groups of huts surrounded by large empty spaces. I soon learnt that one of the huts in each group was to house a battalion HQ staff, another was a cookhouse and another was a store, which when that particular section of the camp was not in use held hundreds of folded bell tents and blankets. It will be realised that, so arranged, this camp was almost infinitely expandable at very short notice. I believe that when full it could accommodate half a million men. There were a collection of huts for the permanent staff, and we occupied some of these. There were also a number of BEF canteens.

At this time thousands of troops were passing through rapidly on their way to and from Germany – those going up being mainly regulars who had signed on for further service. They only stayed one or two nights and our job was to facilitate their passage by putting up tents, providing food and so on. For these duties the battalion was split up into groups, and for most of the time I was there I was in charge of six German prisoners doing the washing up in a huge cookhouse and dining hall. The sergeant cook was a huge jovial man who would have made the perfect 'mine host'. He was always chaffing the German prisoners, who did not really know what he was saying, except one, a corporal who belonged to a very rich family and who was a graduate of Hamburg University. He spoke perfect English and French. This proved to be very useful because a large number of French girls had been recruited to act as waitresses, and as the sergeant could not speak French he could only make his wishes known to most of them by the German corporal consenting to translate. Much amusement was caused by the corporal's attitude to the French girls. He acted as though they had leprosy, and if one of them approached him he would back away as far as he could while still translating. Altogether we had a lot of fun there and, of course, we had the best of food – a matter of very great importance.

I remember Etaples for several other things that happened there. One was that I went on leave to Cheltenham, my first visit home for about a year. Another was the off-duty visits we made to the nearby seaside resort of Le Touquet-Paris-Plage. Then there was the occasion when the battalion was returning from a march over the bridge at the bottom of the camp with Colonel Flanagan riding at the head. Some Australian soldiers were lounging about on the bridge. Though very brave, these Australians were very ill-disciplined and cocky. They liked to take a tilt at all authority. One of them gathered up a snowball and threw it at Colonel Flanagan. It hit him, but the Aussie had picked on the wrong man, for he was instantly pinned against the bridge parapet with the horse's front hooves waving in his face. He looked terrified,

A Norman Fishergirl   *April 18 1919*

Watercolour of a French fisher girl at Le Tréport, from Arthur's 1919 sketchbook (dated 18 April).

especially when Flanagan reached over, took him by the scruff of the neck, yanked him off the ground and threw him full length. His friends, too, looked frightened to death. But everyone roared with laughter when Flanagan made the guilty Aussie take up position in front of his horse and lead the battalion to our camp, about three quarters of a mile distant.

But perhaps the Etaples memory which most affected me was an occasion when I formed part of the guard at (I believe it was) No.4 General Hospital, which I have seen mentioned in histories many times since. I should explain that not only was Etaples a huge camp, but there were huge military hospitals and cemeteries there too.

The portion of the hospital we were guarding was filled with German prisoners and surrounded with barbed wire entanglements. There was no trouble with them, and from the excellent singing which came from the huts (or wards) they seemed very happy; the nurses confirmed that they had no wish to escape. But I was one of a group of six chosen to guard a hut in the corner of the prison hospital. This hut had locked gates and thick barbed wire entanglement within the outer hospital entanglements. We went on guard three at a time for alternate periods of four hours. One sentry, who had the keys of the gates, continually walked round the outside of the barbed wire surrounding the hut, one walked round the hut on the inside, and the third was stationed just inside one door of the hut. We were all given whistles and instructions that at the slightest sign of trouble from any of the inmates we were to shoot to kill. The prisoners knew we had these instructions, for they were all murderers, about thirty of them. Some were awaiting execution and others were awaiting trial. It just so happened that during the waiting period they had to have hospital treatment. Although they had draughts and cards to play with, they kept up a continual barrage of taunts and sneers at the sentry posted inside, and it was as much as he could do to stick it for the one-hour duty period.

The nurses who attended them loathed the job, especially the night nurse. They were accompanied through the ward by the sentry from the inner compound while the sentry at the door covered the nurse and him. The atmosphere in that hut was indescribable. As in all communities, these men had formed themselves into small groups dependent on their degree of education or mutual inclination, and they were at psychological war with one another – and it was all horrible. I was glad when this particular job came to an end.

Then came a day when I was ordered to attend Battalion HQ to be informed that the battalion was leaving Etaples, and I was to be one of an advance party of nine which was to proceed to Le Tréport to take over and allot accommodation in a camp on the top of the cliffs there. The central feature of this camp was a splendidly designed and equipped American hospital with the operating theatre in the centre and the wards radiating from it like the spokes of wheel. We made this our headquarters till the battalion arrived.

Our short stay at Le Tréport was very enjoyable. The sea floor here must have been covered by multicoloured sands, for on a clear day, looking from the cliffs straight down into the sea, it seemed that one was looking at a vast abstract canvas of blues, yellows, reds and greens. The little town nestling at the bottom of the cliffs quite captivated me. It could be reached by the traditional 365 steps or by cliff railway. It was on this railway that Dowsett, a friend of mine, who I regret to say had had too much wine in a Le Tréport estaminet, accidentally sat on a paper bag full of eggs he had purchased for a breakfast treat.

However, my most enjoyable experience during our stay was a route-march which took us to the little town of Eu, which is just inside Normandy and was one of the chief ports from which the army of William the Conqueror embarked for England. Marching through a wood, we suddenly came upon the battlemented walls of the town, which are almost as perfect as in medieval times and just as William must have seen them 900 years ago. We piled arms in the central square. Colonel Flanagan went to a service in the church and we were allowed to explore the town at our leisure.

I can't remember how, when or why we left Le Tréport, but about that time the battalion was ordered to proceed to Palestine to act as bodyguard to Field Marshal Allenby. Everybody under twenty-one was transferred to the 2/5th Glosters and replaced by men over twenty-one from the Glosters who still had some time to serve. The Oxfords departed and the hybrid Glosters found themselves split up and doing various guard duties near the mouth of the Somme. From Abbeville to St Valéry at its mouth, the Somme had been canalised by Napoleon and along this stretch on the west bank there was an ammunition dump, probably one of the biggest ever known: great sheds surrounded by earth banks. I understood the dump was some 17km long and about 2km across. The broad towpath along the river was reached at intervals by

Privates Rush and Nicholls, Arthur's fellow sentries at the post by the river Somme (from his 1919 sketchbook).

Arthur taking a break from duty outside the Nissen hut where he was posted at Harfleur (see sketch on page 99).

roads crossing the dump, and all entrances were guarded by sentry huts, fed from a blockhouse on the other side of the dump. Our platoon occupied the blockhouse, and three of us privates, Rush, Nicholls and myself, were posted to a sentry hut on the river about 5km from the sea. I was supposed to be in charge.

It was very isolated and would have been very lonely but for the fact that it was situated right opposite two emergency timber bridges which the engineers had built against the possibility of retreat, and these were in the process of being dismantled by Chinese Labour Corps who came daily from a camp across the river. Apart from rations delivered by GS wagon we were left very much to our own resources. The local people had special passes to enable them to graze their animals, and one of these became a downright nuisance. She was an attractive peasant girl about sixteen years old, with a pet goat which she would bring to graze on the grass-covered bank between the river and a relief canal parallel to it about fifty yards away.

While we got on very well with the Chinese generally, many of them indulged in brinkmanship by crowding the sentry in his box or reaching out to touch his bayonet – all in jest but very unpleasant. Rush (off duty) came into the hut one day to say that Nicholls was penned in the sentry box. I told him to stay in the hut and cover me in case of trouble, while I went out and frightened them off by levelling the rifle and telling them to 'get out'.

Sometimes if threatened they would call one's bluff by standing and pulling their shirt aside to bare their chests. This was all very worrying, till one day I was standing outside and a 'Chink' – again all in good fun – tried to trip me up from the back. However, I was on the alert for just this sort of thing and having a good knowledge of ju-jitsu (as it was then called) I was able to throw him over my shoulder. This caused a laugh among

Arthur's study of Tchung
Camena Tungwa, who
autographed the drawing
(made in 1919 at Saingeville).
Arthur's caption, 'A Chink',
was the acceptable slang of
the day.

his pals who then crowded round, and pushed forward for 'Plenty fighta fighta'. I was
a bit scared but thought it might be an opportunity to establish some sort of superior-
ity, and telling Rush and Nicholls to shoot if there was any real rough stuff, I took on
three of them in turn. Actually it was very easy meat, for, to my surprise, they were not
very strong and lacked the intelligence to make the most of the uneven ground. When
the little exercise was over I made it clear to them that if there was any more fooling
about I'd rough up the person responsible, and that went for anybody touching the girl
with the goat. We had no more trouble, and in fact I had many invitations to China,
including one to tea in Peking when I was next there! I have a sketch of the gentleman
concerned together with his autograph – 'Tchung Camena Tungwa'[15].

During this period of guard duties there were two other experiences which I think
worth relating. One was a somewhat frightening comedy, and the other a practical
lesson in psychology which was hard to take, but which I now know would have
made the world a much happier and safer place to live in if it had been learnt and
applied by those who make and administer the law.

The comedy (which could have been a tragedy for me) occurred thus wise. The
guard hut, in which we slept, and the sentry box stood on a bank which came to a
corner where the road which crossed the arms dump joined the river towpath. The
sentry box was right on the corner and the hut about eight yards back. To anyone
coming across the dump the sentry box was visible for a quarter of a mile. Rush,
Nicholls and I did sentry duty in turn.

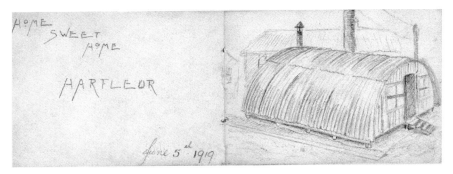

Arthur's sketch of the Nissen hut where he was billeted at Harfleur. His caption, 'Home Sweet Home', is typical of the sense of humour that carried him through many a hardship as well as lighting happy times.

SS *Viking*, from a postcard kept by Arthur, illustrating the type of steamship in use in the early twentieth century. Built in 1881, she was a sealing and whaling vessel and was destroyed by an explosion in 1931 during the making of a film about the industry.

Now, as everyone knows, in war the abandonment of his post by a sentry is punishable by death, and to abandon one's rifle at the same time makes it even more serious (if possible). The war being over, and the fact that apart from those bringing the rations and the visits of the Chinese labourers we didn't see anyone all day, made us a little casual in our attitude to the job. So it was that one day when I was on sentry duty and the ration cart had delivered rations (which included some hot boiled rice and jam in a biscuit tin), and nobody being about, I left my rifle tilted against the sentry box and joined my pals disposing of the rice in the hut. The rice was on a trestle table and I sat on a wooden form. Suddenly Nicholls, who was looking out of the back window, said, 'Scram! There's a group of officers and men coming here and they're about 100 yards away.'

Arthur (front left) with friends from the Gloucestershire Regiment, near Harfleur, *c.* 1919.

Obviously it was too late. They must have already spotted the rifle and the empty sentry box. I wasn't much bothered, as frankly the purpose for which I joined the Army had been achieved, so I thought I'd bluff it out. I therefore went on eating till the party entered the hut. 'Who is supposed to be on duty here?' demanded a second lieutenant, who had joined the battalion after the Armistice and was nicknamed 'One Chevron Dick' because he wore one blue service chevron on his arm (for one year's service). I said, 'I am.' 'Then why are you not at your post?' 'Because I am having my dinner', I replied. This reply was of course insolent, as it was meant to be, for I could not stand the fellow. It made him furious. I didn't mind that, but he did send prickles down my neck when he said 'You are under arrest, for desertion of your post on active service', for I knew then I was in a serious spot. He sent the sergeant back to the blockhouse for an armed guard. He told the officer who was with him to stay with me in the hut till the guard returned. A sentry was placed outside and he himself went off somewhere. Not knowing what else to do, I resumed my dinner, facing the table, while the new officer sat on the same bench facing outwards. I had not really looked at him before, but as I glanced sideways to see what he was like, my heart gave a leap, for I was sure I had met him on a friendly basis somewhere before. But where? I racked my brain desperately and at last I knew, and to get maximum effect I turned to him and said, 'Have you still got that book', (I said the title, which I now forget), 'which I lent you in Norwich?' He looked flabbergasted so I went on, 'Your name is Pike, isn't it, and you were with the 35 TRB in — Street, Norwich.'

'Yes,' he replied, and then, recognising me, he said, 'and your name is Bullock. Fancy meeting you again under these circumstances.' He and I had been friends and both applied for commissions in Norwich. His came through first and he left the battalion before we were rushed to France. He had just come out and was being shown round the different posts. 'Look,' I said, 'Can't you do something about this idiotic position?

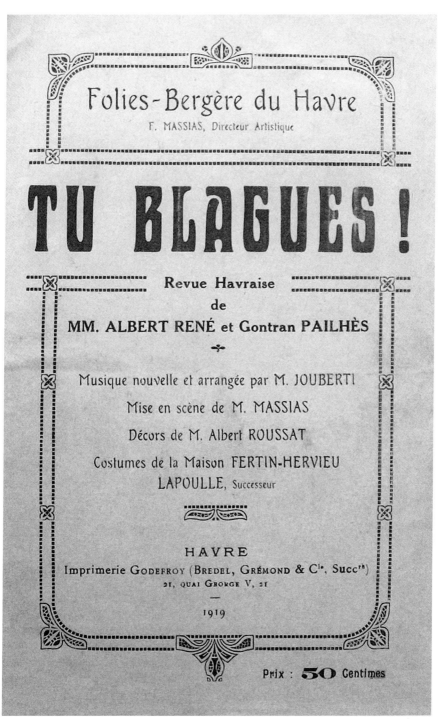

The cover of a programme for a comic revue, *You're Joking!* (1919), which Arthur went to see during his time at Le Havre.

If I'm arrested, there will have to be a court martial even if I'm let off. You'd better go and tell that swollen-headed nincompoop the war is over.'

'Alright,' he said, and off he went to come back in about ten minutes with 'One Chevron', who said, 'Lt Pike has made representation on your behalf as the result of which I will drop the charge, on your promise it will not occur again.'

Needless to say I gave the promise gladly, and when the sergeant marched up with his party he was told to go and march straight back again. Whew! What about that for an escape, and what about that for a coincidence? Could you have one with more odds to one against?

There was little comedy about the other experience. After the 'skilled' Chinese coolies had dismantled the bridges near our post, gangs of other Chinese with armed British NCOs and Chinese NCOs with staves came to remove the material. They were some very rough specimens, and I gathered they had come from a prison camp at Noyelles across the river. It seemed to us that they were treated brutally, so much so that Private Rush personally objected to the action of one officer, who instead of putting Rush on a charge of insolence, as he could have done, explained that these were criminals – some of the lowest characters from the ports of China. They would cut your throat and then look in your pocket to see if it had been worthwhile. He said that murderers were promptly shot (we heard shots from Noyelles every morning) and where there was violence or robbery with violence they got the Noyelles six-week course, and he invited us to see what that meant.

Off duty, we went to a quarry which was not of stone, but just an earth hillside where hundreds of men in tiers were shovelling the face away upwards, where it was filled in to sandbags, carried down, and emptied again and then shovelled up to the top – all seemingly senseless and frustrating. The place was surrounded by armed British NCOs and Chinese policemen with staves. All prisoners were stripped to the waist. No back was supposed to be straightened for fixed periods and no conversation was allowed. Where the rule was broken a Chinese policeman casually walked over and swiped the offender who sometimes was knocked down by the force of the blow.

We expressed the view that it all seemed senseless and ruthlessly brutal and he agreed that it was certainly the latter but not the former, for it was 100 per cent effective. The six-week course meant very hard labour under the strictest discipline, so strict that the slightest breach was physically punished without fail, and the prisoners were deprived of the psychological satisfaction of doing anything useful. The result was that although they had had through their hands some of the most hardened thugs one could imagine, not one had ever been on their books twice. Six weeks at Noyelles and the cure was complete. I recommend it to those responsible for the maintenance of law in this country. It might then be possible for citizens to walk in safety, and for half the prisons to be scrapped.

About June 1919 the Glosters were transferred to the huge hutted camp at Harfleur near Le Havre, and again split up for various base duties. I was one of a group living in a detached Nissen hut, dealing with thousands of troops coming through the transit camp for demobilisation. I have a postcard photo of this worthy bunch, with me on the far left. We had a most enjoyable and carefree time with plenty of food and so on, but our group was not under discipline, and that was fatal. We all became very slack.

Right: 'M'sieur l'Abbé'. A study by Arthur of a French priest, probably at Harfleur.

Below: Arthur's identity pass which he was required to carry during his posting at the important Le Havre base.

IDENTITY PASS, HAVRE BASE, TOWN AND PORT AREA.

No. 5/208 Rank Pte. Name Bullock A S Corps 2/5 Gloucesters

Date: 1.6.19.

Signature:

NOTE.—This pass is only available for one month from date of issue.

M.L.O., HAVRE.

1. 6. 19.

M.L.O. HAVRE.

Cecil Haines for major.
Commanding
M.L.O.

1.7.19
W.S. Lardlethern Capt

One day I was ordered to appear before the company officer, Captain Pope (of whom more anon), for something I had done wrong (but what it was I have not now the remotest idea), and I was ordered back to the battalion. And here occurred one of the most remarkable of the many fateful coincidences in my life.

I think I said earlier that after the Armistice infantrymen not due for demobilisation were asked to volunteer for base jobs. I volunteered for dozens at the same time and took a chance on what came up first. Well, believe it or not, one of these must have come through at the very moment I was being ordered back to the battalion.

When I left Captain Pope I went back to the hut, collected my rifle and gear, slung them over my shoulder and somewhat disconsolately walked along the duckboards to the Gloster huts. Everybody seemed to be out on parade or duty somewhere. I looked into one hut after another, searching for a vacant bed, and at last found a hut obviously only half occupied.

I went in, threw down my gear on an empty bed and sat on the edge of it. To my utter astonishment, at the very moment I did this I heard my name and number being shouted by an orderly coming along the duckboards. I went to the door, stopped him and asked what I was wanted for. He said I was to report to the orderly room, where I would get my instruction and where a lorry was waiting to take me to Le Havre.

I was there before anybody could say 'knife'. I had returned to the battalion for about five minutes and nobody knew I had ever been back. That was my last official contact with the Glosters.

The lorry was taking a number of men to various duties in Le Havre, two of us (both Glosters) being billeted with the staff of No.1 General Post Office (British Army) right at the entrance to Le Havre harbour. (I forget what the name was of my companion, but I will call him Private Evans in a later reference.)

Our billet at No.1 GPO was comfortable, with excellent food cooked and served by German prisoners who were living in comparative luxury and freedom. I was to report for duty the following morning with the AMLO Southampton Quay, and this I did. The full title of this staff officer (with a blue band round his hat) was Assistant Military Landing Officer, Le Havre. He was a captain (from Cheltenham), and his staff consisted of a sergeant of the London Irish and myself, plus a cape boy who generally fetched and carried in a GS wagon. Our office was a temporary wooden one built in the corner of the large Halle des Douanes (Customs Hall), and our job was to vet the passes of military personnel travelling on the civilian packets SS *Hantonia* and SS *Normania*, plying between Le Havre and Southampton, and generally to facilitate the passage of such personnel. One of the packets usually arrived about 8 a.m. and left about midnight. We frequently had supper on board and normally waited for the last train from Paris before authorising departure, in case there were any last-minute passengers. The cape boy took any luggage to and from the station.

We were a very happy family and, although the AMLO was a very important officer with absolute authority, there was no question of rank among us, and we were all on Christian name terms. So long as we were there to deal with the packet in the morning and from about 8 p.m. till departure at midnight, we were free to do as we pleased, and I spent many happy hours exploring Le Havre and district – which I grew quite fond of.

More studies from
Arthur's 1919
sketchbook: (left)
Harfleur Church, and
(below) a French airship
over Le Havre (dated
6 August).

From the GPO to the office was about half a mile along the quay, the Southampton Quay being the portion to the west of where the Rue de Paris comes out onto the harbour. The quarter of the city lying between the Rue de Paris and the Southampton Quay was the 'red lamp' district. It was out of bounds to British troops, and practically every day I was there a dead body was pulled out of the water. As a result I did not much enjoy my walk alone at midnight back to the billet.

My period of duty here was a wonderful and unique experience because it coincided with the great Peace Conference at Versailles, which meant that many famous statesmen, generals and admirals, all travelling on military passes, went through our hands. If only I had kept an autograph album it would have been priceless today. It would take too long to mention them all, but there is one instance I must relate.

I had had my supper on board and was reading a book on the blanket-covered trestle table (which formed our desk) while waiting for the last train from Paris. The AMLO was aboard, flirting with some lady passengers. Suddenly the office was filled with two very big 'brass hats' of high rank, who must have come by car. One of them gave me two yellow passes, the top one of which bore the name Colonel Pitt Taylor. I did not look at the other, as only the AMLO could deal with yellow passes; I handled the green ones. I explained this to them and said the AMLO was aboard and would be back in a few minutes. I resumed my reading, but out of the corner of my eye saw Pitt Taylor lounge back against the wall of the office, while the other very tall man blocked the doorway by putting his feet against the one jamb and lying back against the other.

The minutes ticked on, and I was beginning to get worried, when the AMLO appeared outside the door. He sprang to attention, saluted, rushed into the office, grabbed the yellow passes and disappeared with the officers. Some time later he returned, sank into a chair and wiped his brow. I said, 'What's the matter? I have never seen you salute anybody before.' He asked, 'How long have they been here?' I replied, 'About twenty minutes.'

He nearly threw a fit, and the rest of the conversation is not fit to record, except that he said, 'Don't you know who you have been entertaining?' I replied, 'Colonel Pitt Taylor.' When he said 'Colonel Pitt Taylor is the aide-de-camp of Field Marshal Sir Henry Wilson', I realised that my lanky guest in the doorway, to whom I had not even offered a seat, was the Chief of Staff of the British Army, head of all our military forces. Perhaps I can excuse my lapse by explaining that so many 'brass hats' were passing through at the time that they were 'two-a-penny.'

While attached to the AMLO staff I was granted leave in England, and this proved to be an unforgettable experience for several reasons. Because of my relations with the cross-channel packet staff I wangled a free passage in comfort with a sleeping bunk on the SS *Hantonia* to Southampton. To my surprise and delight, when I awoke in the morning we were passing up Spithead through hundreds of Allied warships assembling for the victory review.

Some ten days later on my return journey I arrived in Paddington at about 2 a.m. Cars were always available to take soldiers from one terminus to the other during the night, and the driver of my car, learning I had not got to arrive at Waterloo before 8 a.m., suggested we made a grand tour of the route for the Allied victory march due to take place the next day. So I had the unique experience of traversing that route

The cover of an early colour guide book to Le Havre, published in 1913, which Arthur used during his time stationed there.

A moment of relaxation with friends. Arthur starts up a gramophone that he acquired while posted at Le Havre base, 1919.

through almost completely empty streets, all lit up like a ballroom for my enjoyment. But that was not all. There were only about fifty soldiers on the boat out of Southampton, so we had the full run of the vessel, with extra rations, on a beautiful day for cruising, and on the way from Southampton we passed along the route to be taken by the Royal Yacht in a couple of days' time, right down the serried ranks of the greatest assembly of war vessels the world had ever seen or is ever likely to see again.

Unfortunately, all good things come to an end, and so did my halcyon life at Le Havre. The trouble was that I had been too clever, for when I had seen the notices on the battalion notice board, offering cushy base jobs to infantrymen, I applied for them all. The AMLO job was one, and another was the Royal Army Ordnance Corps; unfortunately my transfer to the RAOC came through just when I was beginning to enjoy the Army. So off I had to go to join the staff of the greatest military supply base in history, between Le Havre and Harfleur.

We lived in a camp of Nissen huts surrounded by barbed wire and guarded by French civilians with guard dogs. The reason for so much protection was that, although the base was under heavy military guard, there were raids nearly every night by armed gangs intent on stealing supplies. When I tell you that on one occasion a sentry of the King's Royal Rifles killed five Arabs out of a gang which was raiding across the canal at Soquence, you will understand how serious the situation was.

Arthur (second from left at the back) and the staff of T Group at Le Havre base, 1919. The jaunty angle of the picture reflects Arthur's comment that 'there never was a happier office staff'.

I was attached to 'T' Group Office, which controlled stores of clothing in an immense hangar or warehouse. Other similar warehouses contained everything one can think of for conducting a war. All the books were stores books recording goods in and goods out, and, of course, there were no money values to be considered or dealt with. The 'T' Group office staff consisted of a captain, a lieutenant, one conductor, one sub-conductor (as they call warrant officers in the RAOC), one sergeant, about three privates (male clerks) and about four WAAC privates (female clerks) under the control of a WAAC sergeant, Miss Trigg.

There never was a happier office staff than we were. I forget the name of the captain, but he was known to everybody as 'the Bacon Stasher' because apparently in civilian life he had been a manager for the Co-op at West Hartlepool. Of course there was plenty of fooling about, but I want to emphasise that it was all good, clean fun, which would not have made the Archbishop of Canterbury blush.

Arthur working with Babs Robertson at Le Havre. Babs allegedly had a 'crush' on Arthur but he remembered her chiefly for sharing her shortbread!

One of the WAACs, Babs Robertson from Scotland, developed rather a crush on me. She was extremely nice, and the shortbread from home which she shared with me was delicious, but I'm afraid it was a case of unrequited love as I had a girl at home in Cheltenham. I wonder what became of her?

All the labouring in the base was done by Chinese coolies and German prisoners, and there was no love lost between them. A German would not stand anywhere near a coolie and would spit on the ground if he had to pass one.

The coolies were inefficient, and dreadful thieves. The Germans were well-behaved, hard-working and conscientious. They were allowed a lot of licence and were provided with sports gear for inter-hut competitions. They didn't attempt to run away, as they were being gradually released and in the meantime were having a better time than they would be having back home.

With the ending of hostilities, supplies were being withdrawn from the front and being sent to the various bases in enormous quantities. Here, selected stores were being shipped to England, and the rest was sold in daily auction sales or burnt. To give you some idea of quantities involved, there was an open field several acres in extent completely covered by expensive machining tools with only walking space between them. Then there were thousands of miles of barbed wire, millions of blankets, thousands of motorbikes and so on. The buyers were mostly French, and as their purchases were loaded onto lorries by German prisoners or Chinese coolies the purchaser would often give the NCO in charge a fifty franc note not to be too careful in checking the quantity loaded! Next to the base, Schneiders were building a shipyard for which they wanted labour, and some of the NCOs, having collected their labour squads in the morning, marched them to the boundary, where they were handed over to Schneiders foremen, who in return handed back sufficient francs to make the risk worthwhile.

Pilfering of stores was universal by all ranks. My laundry was done by a Frenchwoman living by Harfleur church, and I always paid her with a pair of corduroy trousers, which she could flog without difficulty for more than the cost of the laundry.

Gradually the stores and size of staff were reduced, until only a small number were left to clear up. Major Gay was in command of the base, and he established himself in the 'T' Group Office. Under his instructions I was ordered to get all the books of the base together and transfer the balances into one set, for simplification and writing off. This was a big job, and Major Gay (who I believe was a stockbroker in 'civvy' life) was most anxious to finish the job and get back home. I had another leave due, but he said if I would forego that leave for his sake, he would arrange with the powers that be that I could be demobbed that much earlier, in fact as soon as the job was done. I agreed to this, as he seemed to be able to pull strings in the necessary quarters.

So the day came when all stock was cleared and all balances collated and written off. I remember very well the last time I closed the last book and thought to myself, 'By this action I am closing the greatest military base there has ever been on earth.' And so it was.

Major Gay left. The gates of the base were closed, and an office-cum-orderly room was established inside the camp containing living quarters. This was occupied by a lieutenant who had come to replace Major Gay, a sub-conductor and myself. The total staff, including us three, was fifteen. I explained my position to the lieutenant (whose name I forget), and he promised to find out what arrangements Major Gay had made for my release. He reported that no one knew of any arrangements. I pointed out that services at the base voluntarily undertaken by infantrymen between the Armistice and the date when they were due for demobilisation were not to delay that demobilisation, and as mine was due I regarded myself as relieved of all military duties and I would accept no more commands, nor would I do one more stroke of work, but as I was being illegally detained in the Army against my will they would have to pay the cost of keeping me till I was released. In other words I established a one-man mutiny. I told the lieutenant I wanted facilities to contact my MP. He didn't know what to do and took the path of least resistance by accepting the position. I got in touch with my MP in Cheltenham, Mr Agg Gardner, and asked for his assistance. He tackled the War Office, then presided over by Mr Winston Churchill, and got a reply from Churchill's Parliamentary Private Secretary, Lord Wodehouse (I believe), quoting a War Office order justifying my retention. I replied that Wodehouse didn't know what he was talking about and quoted a War Office order which had replaced his, and which

The 'tricouleur' cover of a jotter which Arthur bought in France in 1919, light-heartedly alluding to the alliance between France and England.

justified my position (I have all this correspondence somewhere among my records). I don't know what Agg Gardner did, but within a few days I was called to the office to be shown a telegram received by the lieutenant, instructing that all personnel at the camp not signed on for future service were to be released at once and proceed to Fovant for demobilisation. Everybody was delighted, though they had all previously expressed the view that I was banging my head against a brick wall.

So off we went via Boulogne and Dover. But I must just mention that Channel crossing. It was awful. The sea was boiling and the ship was flung about all over the place. The main trouble was that it had a terrible roll, and as we entered Dover harbour we nearly capsized. The vessel was crowded with soldiers on all decks, and each was loaded with kit. When Dover came in sight all were standing up in anticipation of landing. Just as the prow passed the harbour wall, the ship was hit by a terrific wave curling along the wall. This turned her over to starboard so that the gunwales were awash, and the lurch threw hundreds of soldiers and their kit over to that side in a great heap. It seemed ages before she swung back on to an even keel – inside the harbour, thank goodness. I may add that at almost the same time as we arrived in Dover, a destroyer from Calais also arrived, bringing Mr W.H. Hughes, Prime Minister of Australia. He had some ribs broken on a locker on the way over!

However, all's well that ends well, and, greatly relieved, we landed safely at Dover, where we entrained for our demobilisation centre at Fovant – of happy memories. There, on 13 December 1919, I received my demobilisation papers and again became a private citizen after two years and five months in the Army, one year and seven months of which had been spent on active service in France. My feelings as I took the train to Cheltenham were an indescribable mixture which I will not attempt to analyse.

Seven

Penury and Perseverance

Scrooge had a very small fire,
but the clerk's fire was so very much smaller
that it looked like one coal.

(Charles Dickens, *A Christmas Carol*)

The house in Cheltenham to which I returned, and which I was to regard as a temporary home, was 4 Pitville Lawn, one of a Georgian terrace block of five overlooking Pitville Gardens. It was a high-class apartment house of which my eldest sister Alice was the very efficient landlady, and our sister Florence her able partner and assistant. Mother still occupied the rooms near Alice and lent her a hand in return for meals, but her maintenance was to become a problem in view of the fact that her allowance from the Army had ceased with my demobilisation.

All went well for a time, but my sisters' temperaments were very different and their partnership became more and more uneasy. Florence, though efficient, detested domestic service and had ambitions to become a Deaconess in the Church of England. Alice was receiving correspondence from a David Merretti, to whom she had been engaged before her marriage to Harry Hall, and who had gone out to North America to make his fortune. David had learned that she was now free, and the purport of his letters was that he should return to England and marry her. In the outcome that is what happened, and Floss (as I will call her hereafter) left to join the Church. Alice carried on the business after Floss's departure, but it was doomed. It was difficult for Dave to fit into a society mainly of women (many of them old maids with a limited outlook), having come direct from managing a huge wheat farm in North Dakota where all the staff were men – and roughnecks at that. As for Floss, while her departure was disastrous for the business she made a successful career for herself in the Church, especially in connection with Sunday school reform[16].

So far I have not mentioned my relations with the opposite sex, and perhaps I ought to say a word or two on the subject. In spite of the fact that I had four sisters and went to a mixed school with a fair cross-section of girls, I have always regarded them as being made of superior clay, and been a little shy of them. When I was at school I was constantly teased about sweethearts, which in fact I never had, and it is true that until I was seventeen I had only been for a walk with two girls, Freda Burns and Gwen Hawker, neither of whom I had had the courage to kiss, but shortly before

I joined up, while staying with Alice in Cheltenham, I volunteered to become a Sunday school teacher at St Peter's where Floss and her friends were trying an experiment in reformed teaching methods. There I met and became attracted to another teacher, Miss Minnie Allen. I don't seem to have been very suited for this kissing business, for the first time I ventured to attempt a goodnight kiss on the doorstep in Swindon Road, on a wet blustery night, the collar of my Mac blew between our faces and I kissed her through the flap. Undeterred by this setback, Miss Allen and I spent some time together; we corresponded during my Army service and she was there to meet me on my return.

It was very welcome to have a few weeks' holiday on my war gratuity (during which time I had the pleasure of seeing the great ballet dancer Pavlova and her company give a performance at Cheltenham Town Hall), but I had to think of the future. This presented quite a problem, with millions of men coming back on to the labour market. The government offered many training courses, for which subsistence grants were made. Professional men were asked to take on trainees whose wages during training would be paid by the government. I decided to try civil engineering.

I became a trainee in the office of Mr H.C. James Carrington MIME, MCI, AMIEE, who described himself as a consulting engineer and works architect. At the same time I took a three-year correspondence course with the College of Estate Management, London, under two tutors, both of whom were members of the Institute of Civil Engineering. As the result of this training I hoped to sit the necessary examination to become a member of that institution also. The course included a revisionary syllabus in general subjects – especially mathematics, applied mechanics and physics – plus the theory of structures, strength of materials, hydraulics, general surveying and quantity surveying.

I remember the day I started with Mr Carrington standing at the bottom of Hill Street, seeing the buildings of central Birmingham towering above me and wondering just what we were going to mean to one another in the next few years. Actually I came to have quite an affection for 'good old Brum', but that is more than I can say for Mr Carrington. It was not long before I realised that for him I was a form of cheap labour; that he suffered from an inferiority complex arising from a lack of engineering theory (though he had a lot of practical knowledge and experience); that he was highly suspicious; that owing to a lack of jobs coming through he was struggling to make ends meet; and that he spent far too much time attending or organising Free Masonry functions.

Apart from Mr Carrington and myself, the staff consisted of a typist named Miss Hill and another pupil named Parkes. His father had paid a premium of £200 for him and he only received a nominal wage, but his father was well able to afford to keep him as he was head of a big building firm at Halesowen and a director of the West Bromwich Football Club. Sometimes, on a Friday, Parkes would ask if I was doing anything on Saturday as if not I could have his sister's season ticket because she would not be going to the match. So on several Saturday afternoons I could be found seated in the directors' box at the Hawthorns.

I found it very hard-going, working all day and studying every evening, until I decided to do no work on Saturdays and I went to either a soccer or a rugby match in the afternoons. For a time I used to watch Moseley Rugby Club playing at the Reddings and later I played for the newly formed Hall Green Rugby Club. At that time a trade fair used to be held for six months every year at the Bingley Hall (off Broad Street), where on Saturday afternoons I could get several hours of very cheap entertainment and hear one of the best bands or orchestras, playing in time with a huge illuminated fountain. I suppose I must have heard all the best civilian and military bands in the country.

On Saturday evenings I went to the pictures, to the international celebrity concerts at the Town Hall or to a dance. At the suggestion of my cousin, Elsie Clifford (who was personal secretary to the founder of Kunzles, the chocolate and confectionery firm), I joined a group of young men and girls of about my own age who belonged to St Gregory's Church Institute. We made up quite a large party who frequently went to dances all over Birmingham – at the Grand Hotel, the Imperial Hotel or the Fiveways Assembly Rooms. They were a middle-class cross-section and the jolliest people imaginable. It would take too long to report all the funny things that happened to us, but it is worth recording that although they were as lively a bunch as one could wish to meet, during all the time I was with them their conduct was beyond reproach. I was very sorry when circumstances parted us.

At the celebrity concerts I saw many of the greatest stars of the period, including the great Russian bass Chaliapin on the first visit he was allowed to make outside Russia after the Revolution. He had the most commanding appearance, being big, tall and handsome, with the most colossal opinion of himself. The advertisement in the *Birmingham Post* referred to him as 'the great Russain basso', and he wrote demanding that it should be altered to the 'great Russian singer', for, he said, 'I can sing anything.' His chief songs were the 'Volga Boatsong' and 'The Song of the Flea'. In the latter, the dramatic effect is enhanced by slight pauses after the word 'flea', followed by 'ha ha ha ha ha'. He came to one of these pauses and sang as loudly as possible, 'a flea – ', and stopped for effect. At that moment the bell of the clock of the Council House (100 yards away) went 'Bang!' with the first strike of 9 o'clock, and about 1,500 people, including Chaliapin, exploded in laughter. Shortly afterwards, singing something with the greatest noise he could possibly make, he lifted up his right arm grasping a length of wood several feet long which, in the intensity of his effort, he had torn off the cover of the grand piano.

Mr Carrington's office was on the top floor of Winchester House, Victoria Square, Birmingham. Winchester House was a very fine if somewhat ornate block of offices, which I was disappointed to find on my last visit to Birmingham had been demolished to facilitate the movement of traffic. It stood exactly opposite the Council House and I could look straight in to the banqueting hall and adjacent rooms on the second floor where important visitors were entertained, and I had a wonderful view of all the civic ceremonies. The most interesting of these was the granting of the Freedom of the City to David Lloyd George. He was accompanied by his daughter Megan, and just before the ceremony, which was to take place in the Town Hall on the opposite side of Victoria Square, they appeared through the curtains of the window of the retiring room allotted to them next to the banqueting hall. From his gestures, he was obviously telling Megan of the famous evening years before when, after speaking at the Town Hall, he had to escape from a hostile mob by dressing as a policeman and marching off with a squad. Both he and Megan were in fits of laughter. Another notable occasion was the visit of Edward, Prince of Wales, later Edward VIII.

Arthur training in civil
engineering in Carrington's
offices, overlooking Victoria
Square in Birmingham, 1922.

After about a year Parkes, having finished his training, left and I became Carrington's sole assistant. Using Carrington's patent system of reinforced concrete construction I designed the headquarters of Frederick Burgess (Britain's largest retail agricultural engineers) at Green Lane, Stafford. I helped design factories for Chubb (safe makers) and for E.W. Bliss (tin can makers); also a novel furniture depository to accommodate pantechnicons on racks.

I remember two cases where we were called in as expert witnesses. One was on behalf of a drop-stamping firm working next to a bottling store, and the other on behalf of a cartage firm, some of whose horses had strayed and been killed by a motorist on the highway. In the first case we had to show by technical argument and diagrams that the considerable loss being suffered by the bottling company through bottles of wine falling off the shelves could not possibly have been caused by vibration from the operation of the drop stamps. Obviously this was a pretty difficult, if not impossible, job. Carrington realised this, and I'm afraid I made matters worse, and mortally offended him, when, as we were going up the steps of the Law Courts in Corporation Street, I said I had recently read that there were three kinds of liars, 'ordinary liars, damned liars, and expert witnesses'. We lost the case because the judge took the simple and common sense course of adjourning the court and going to the bottling store, where he stood while the drop stamps were operated. In the second case further offence was given to Carrington (who had no sense of humour) when

I temporarily incorporated into my drawing of horses across the car bonnet a picture of Uncle Tom Cobley's old grey mare with its paws on the bonnet making rude remarks to the driver. We lost that action too, on the simple plea that the horses had no business on the road in the first place.

All the reference books and catalogues were kept in Carrington's office. I was bound to consult them but if I did so in his absence he would not speak to me for days. One day he was trying to fit a bulb over the typist's desk but could not get it right. I asked if I might try, so I caught hold of it and by luck it went in first time. I jokingly said, 'What one needs is the magic touch.' Carrington flung out of the room in fury and did not speak to me for a week. I mention these trivial incidents to indicate what a small-minded man he was. The climax came when we got an order from Hall Bros, the steel stockists, to produce for them the tables for beams and stanchions for a handbook of steel sections to cover a new generation of these sections. Carrington was delighted. Hall Bros wanted this handbook to be produced before any of their competitors', and Carrington had promised to let them have all the performance tables during the following week. On hearing this I told him it was impossible and it might take weeks to produce them. He was very angry. We started working independently.

One day when he was out I had to consult a reference book in his office, and in doing so I saw one of these tables half-finished on a drawing board. At a glance I could see it was all wrong. All the answers were coming out as whole figures whereas about twenty-nine out of thirty should have been decimals. I was in a quandary. If I told him I had visited his office and could not help seeing the table, he would regard it as gross impertinence and unwarranted intrusion. If I did not speak to him about it he would go on wasting time and money and the fact that it was all wrong would have to come out sometime under circumstances even more embarrassing. I had no option but to tell Carrington as gently and politely as I could that he was not working the tables out correctly. To my surprise, he did not become angry but merely asked to see the formulae I was using to see if they were better than his, as though there could be two kinds of truth! These formulae were the ones on which the calculations had to be worked out for a given steel section or combination of sections to give the basic performance figures over different lengths. Having seen my formulae he suggested I should work out the key figures and he would then use those figures for the load calculation for the different lengths using his circular slide rule. In other words, I was to do the skilled technical work and he would do the donkey work. We finally produced the necessary tables before anyone else, but it took us weeks and Carrington never forgave me for saving his business reputation.

It was while checking various formulae in connection with this job that I discovered and reported an error in the formulae given in the *Encyclopedia Britannica*. They wrote back to thank me and to explain that it was almost unheard of to find a mistake in this publication as hundreds of technical readers were used to eliminate them.

At the end of each of the three years I was with Carrington, he was supposed to send a report to the Army as to my progress. I do not know what he said in the first one but the second was so damning that I was instructed to appear before a panel of officers to decide if my grant should be continued. I cannot now remember what

Young women friends from St Gregory's Social Club, Birmingham, with whom Arthur enjoyed many happy dances and days out. This was photographed in 1922. On the right is his cousin, Elsie Clifford.

I was accused of but the chairman of the panel of five 'read me the Riot Act' in big way. I was dumbfounded by the venom Carrington had put into the report and just waited until the storm was over. Having finished his speech, the chairman said, 'You don't seem to be taking any notice of what I have been saying, but from the smile on your face you think I have been talking through the top of my hat.' To this I replied, having nothing to lose by sticking up for myself, 'That is exactly what I was thinking', at which the panel nearly collapsed. I said, 'I've listened to you, now you listen to me', and I told them just what I thought about Carrington and all his works, winding up with the statement that the report was unjustified vindictive rubbish. They could believe me or not as they thought fit, and as far as I was concerned they and Carrington could go to hell. The effect was dramatic. The chairman asked me not to take it so much to heart and admitted that they had felt the report was bound to be an exaggeration. He asked who had been my battalion commander when I was demobbed, and when I said Colonel Flanagan of the East Surreys the meeting broke up into a discussion of that extraordinary officer. I left the room smoking one of the chairman's cigarettes, his arm across my shoulder and an assurance that I could forget the whole thing. I have on many occasions since wondered why I was asked the question about my battalion commander, and thanked my lucky stars it was Colonel Flanagan.

The first part of my stay in Birmingham was spent in lodgings, first in a road in Sparkhill off the Stratford Road, and then, because my landlady was going to have a baby, I was taken over by her sister, Mrs Shuttleworth, who lived in a cosy cul-de-sac just off the Moseley Road. They had never had a lodger before. This was a very lucky move for me because Mrs Shuttleworth had a diploma in domestic science and was anxious to exercise her skill. Her husband only liked a limited range of foods, and those of the plainest; and her small son also was no gourmet. She welcomed me with open arms when she learnt that I was fond of every sort of food but black puddings, so every day became a feast day. She would take no payment for days I was away and once, when I insisted on paying for something, she bought a set of stiff collars (then in fashion) and put them on the breakfast table. She even remade a suit of mine which was becoming shabby by turning it inside out. I also got on well with her husband, who was a somewhat colourless conscientious socialist and a skilled electric wire-man. Mrs Shuttleworth was intuitive to the point of clairvoyance, and I often had the impression that she knew what I was thinking before I spoke. The culmination of this was the occasion when I had to tell her that I should be leaving to set up house for my mother, and she calmly said she fully understood as she had known the circumstances for some time (actually she had this information from a friend, whose husband knew my father).

The Cheltenham boarding house having been given up, I was my mother's only financial supporter because in reply to a circular my brother and sisters had all had made excuses and declined to contribute to her maintenance. So I had to get rooms for us both on my very limited training allowance. We took two rooms with a Mr and Mrs Adams, at 27, Pasey Road, Sparkhill. My mother had the bedroom, and I slept in the sitting room. Cooking facilities were shared. We got on fairly well but it was very difficult. Mother was not used to a big city and could not really adapt herself, especially as we had very little money to spare. My activities were severely curtailed. Fortunately life was made a little pleasanter by the people next door with whom we struck up a friendship; they had us in frequently to play cards, and we often stayed to tea or supper.

It was during this period that I began to feel I was for some reason or other up against a malevolent fate, and I remembered something Lucy had said when reading my character from handwriting. She was exceptionally good at this, but would never do it for relatives or someone she knew very well. However, one day I persuaded her to. Halfway through she broke off and said, 'I have found out something about you that I would not have expected. It does not matter how hard you work or how clever you are, you will always manage to live fairly comfortably, but you will never make much money or be well off, and there is nothing you can do about it.'[17]

Now there is no one I despise more than the man who explains his lack of fortune by whining about ill-luck when everyone knows it was the result of incompetence or laziness, but I know from bitter experience that luck is one of the very real factors in the life of everyone. Things too numerous to list began to go wrong for me, some important and some trivial, which could have no explanation but luck. I will mention two or three to illustrate what I mean. I have explained that Carrington and I did not get on very well, partly because we were not on the same wavelength, and I was not very happy. It was against this background that the incidents I mention began to occur.

I have mentioned that from my office window I could see into and right across the Banqueting Hall of the Council House. One day Princess Mary, daughter of George V, was given the Freedom of the City. I had a Brownie Kodak box camera, with which I took several pictures of the reception and ceremony. I took the film to a chemist to have it developed and printed. When I called for it the chemist said there was nothing on the film and asked me to take the camera in for examination. This I did, and called again for the explanation. Imagine my surprise when he produced a celluloid cover from the end of a folding collar stud (common at the time) and told me that he found this wedged into the small recess at the back of the lens on the inside of the camera. It exactly fitted the recess and permitted no light to come through. I had never had such a collar stud and as far as I could remember the camera had not been accessible to anyone who would have been likely to – or likely to have dreamt of – using it in this way. The possibilities were extremely limited. The incident is trivial and apparently pointless, but the more one thinks of it the more incredible it becomes, so much so that I am forced to the defensive remark that it must be true because I am quite incapable of dreaming up anything so absurd.

I became a member of a professional engineering organisation, and one day we were advised that Senator Marconi would meet us at the Town Hall on a certain date to talk to us and explain the original apparatus used by him in the development of wireless. This was regarded as a great and unique occasion for which the admission would be by invitation cards. I duly received my card, but I did not meet Marconi, for although posted a week before, it arrived two days late![18]

We used to take that famous weekly journal, *John Bull*, and one day they sponsored a jigsaw puzzle in which the cardboard pieces, red on one side and grey on the other, could be put together to form a five-point star. A prize of £250 was offered for a red star arranged like the master in their offices, £150 for an alternative, and £100 for one half red and half grey. I bought one and spent the evening trying to solve it. Mother went to bed and asked how long I should be. I said I was staying up till I had solved it. This I did at about one o'clock in the morning. I then solved the alternatives. However, it occurred to me that if I could do it so easily, others would too, and the prizes would have to be divided. The only thing to do was to ensure that I had a large number of the division. So the next morning I went into Stanford and Mann's in New Street with all the money I could scrape up and bought their whole stock of puzzles, much to the astonishment of the manager. These I took home and spent the evenings for several days pasting the completed puzzles onto cardboard. I then sent them with the postage to my relations and friends telling them to sign and send them in and send the prizes to me, less a certain discount. All these people received a prize but me. Some sent the agreed amount of money on to me and some didn't. A list was published of the prize winners and they were all included except me. I was very considerably out of pocket.

I said we were friendly with our neighbours on one side but this was not true of our neighbours on the other side. Quite the contrary. They were particularly objectionable and, for some reason, very inquisitive about our affairs. They had assumed that Mother was a widow, and she did not advise them otherwise, nor did we tell our friends or the Adamses more of our business than was necessary. One day I was forced to write to my father to say that he was several weeks in arrears with the small weekly contribution he made for Mother's upkeep, and that it was too small anyway and should be increased. He replied with a letter I would not have liked anyone to read, in which the situation was made clear in the worst possible terms. That letter, though properly addressed, was the only one I can remember having been delivered in error to the undesirable neighbours, who opened it, read it and passed it to us. What it contained was made known to the Adamses and to our friends next door.

It was during this period too that my affairs of the heart took a turn for the worse. I have already mentioned my association with Minnie Allen. This continued during my period in Birmingham and I used to go to Cheltenham for the weekend about once a month (it was very cheap). At that time she was working at Cheltine[19] Foods as a typist, and one of her workmates was a Miss Olive Savory. Both of them were in a group of young women who worshipped (or had a 'pash' on) Miss Doris Dent, sister of Phyllis the Sunday school reformer, who was mainly instrumental in my sister Florence taking a career in the Church. How strong this 'pash' became is evidenced by the fact that Doris Dent decided to go to live in London to get rid of it, but Miss Savory found out where she was gone, gave up her job and went to live near Miss Dent in London. It would hardly be an exaggeration to say that several of these girls or young women (some of them domestic servants) had had their heads turned to a point where they were in danger of becoming religious maniacs. When Mother came to live with me I went to Cheltenham much less frequently and each time found Minnie in a highly religious emotional state, which led to misunderstanding and bickering. Some of what she was beginning to believe was plain rubbish so we decided to discuss our differences in the presence of Father Lara, who was head of the English Sunday School Union. I had been attending church less and less frequently, but at the suggestion of Lara I agreed to go regularly to St Agatha's church, Birmingham, where the rector was the greatest preacher of the day. He was a converted Jew named Rosenthal and was at that time in the middle of his famous quarrel with Bishop Barnes over the reservation of the Sacrament. The church held 1,100 people but because of his fame as a preacher and his notorious quarrel with his bishop, one had to get to the church at least half an hour before time to stand a chance of getting a seat; and hundreds were turned away at every service. There is no doubt about Rosenthal's ability to preach, but I began to suspect that he was not altogether sincere in what he said and was indulging in a good deal of showmanship. So one evening I stayed behind and challenged him regarding one of his sermons. He invited me to dine with him during the week and this was followed by a discussion in which I accused him of playing to the gallery. To my surprise he took it in good part and frankly admitted it, but went on to claim that it was necessary to draw and hold the crowds and he was thus doing far more good than he would be by preaching to an empty church.

That more or less finished the experiment for me and cancelled my promise. My visits to church became less frequent and Minnie got more and more caught up. So we drifted apart. Then for a change I invited her to Birmingham for the weekend, going to a lot of trouble to find accommodation. She was to wait for me under the clock on New Street Station. I was unavoidably a few minutes late. She was not there, and I did not know what to do. She had decided to find the way herself, but, not knowing Birmingham, had got lost, arriving hours late. The weekend was not a success, and the conditions under which I was living were not very bright, so I decided in both our interests to call it a day. I was very sorry to do this as she was an exceptionally nice girl.

My training period with Carrington came to an end in March 1923, and I applied to the Institute of Civil Engineers for permission to sit for the AMICE. The forms were returned to me, with a letter to say I could not sit as my training did not comply with the rules of the institution, which state that the practical training must be with

Arthur's mother, Sarah, in old age. Since she had taken the justifiable (but then unusual) step of leaving her husband, she was in a vulnerable position. After returning from the war, Arthur supported her as best he could, sharing lodgings and his meagre training allowance with her while he was apprenticed in Birmingham.

and under a member of the institution, and Mr Carrington, with all his letters and qualifications, was not a member. It was pointed out to them that my tutors at the College of Estate Management were both members, but it was no use. They still refused, and this was the greatest disappointment of my life.

Of course I was trained up to that point in mathematics, physics, applied mechanics, hydraulics, steel construction, general building, concrete construction, general survey-ing and quantity surveying, and in the ordinary way this would have been sufficient to secure a first-class job, particularly as I had considerable business experience, which I had reinforced with an accountancy course with Bennett College of Sheffield. But we were at the beginning of the Great Depression, when literally no buildings were being ordered at all, and no work was coming into the office. Carrington kept me on to com-plete work already in hand but he really could not afford to do so, although I was the only draughtsman in the office. I was expecting to have to leave, but the manner of my dismissal was typical of the man. I had arranged to spend my week's holiday at Weston-super-Mare with Mother and my cousin, Laura Gifford. In my wages envelope for the week preceding the holiday I found a note with my holiday pay to give me a week's notice – the week being, of course, the holiday week which he could not avoid paying.

I was terribly shocked and worried, as I did not know what I was going to do about Mother on my return. I could not spoil her holiday and Laura's by telling them, so I acted as normally as possible and only broke the news to her on our return.

Some of Arthur's technical drawing equipment, including (above) Bakelite set squares, his slide rule and a calculating machine, and (below) his set of compasses and calipers.

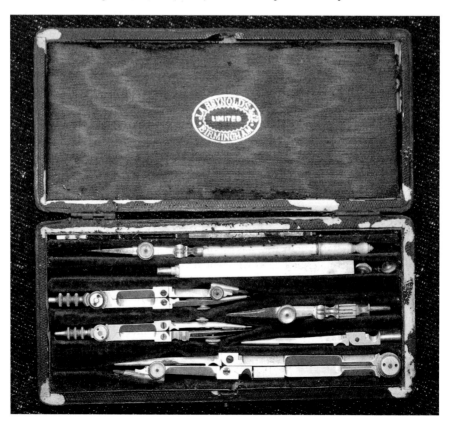

I tried to get a job, but it was quite hopeless. Architects, accountants and engineers were 'two-a-penny' and were glad to get a job at 50 shillings a week. I wrote hundreds of letters, orthodox and unorthodox, but in vain, until one day I received a reply from the managing director of Bristol Motors of Bristol Road, Birmingham, asking me to call. I did this, full of hope. He told me to sit down and then said, 'The two jobs you applied for are both filled, but I felt I just had to see the chap who wrote the letters you sent.' My heart went into my boots and I was very angry, but he went on to say he understood the position fully and because of my letters he would create a job for me in a sausage factory at Dudley, of which he was managing director. It would be well-paid, but there would be no promotion. He added that he gathered from my letters that I was ambitious and highly qualified, but that was the best he could do and he felt I might not accept. I said, 'I will think it over and let you know.' He replied that he was sorry, but I would have to decide there and then. He would give me one minute.

At the end of the minute he said, 'Well?' and I said, 'Thank you, but I can't accept.'

His response was, 'Good for you. I didn't expect you to. All I can recommend is that as you look pretty strong you get a job with a spade, with one of the contractors putting in underground cables for the National Electric Grid, and do your best. It won't be long before someone will call you up out of the trench for something better. You will then have got your foot in the door, and it will be up to you.'

Just to indicate the state of unemployment at the time I must report that he said they had received thousands of applications. He indicated two sacks of unopened letters and said there were more at the post office which they had been instructed not to deliver.

Very depressed and dejected, I wrote to all members of the family, telling them the position and that I could not support Mother any more. They had not been very helpful all the time she had been with me, and there was no great rush to help in this crisis. I can't remember all the details but finally Mr John Gay, to whom Lucy was acting as a sort of companion and secretary and whom she later married, made it financially possible for Lucy and Mother to set up house in a flat in Cromwell Road, Bristol. It was a wonderful gesture which I accepted with the greatest relief.

I was determined not to go on the dole in Birmingham if I could help it, but I was now nearly broke. However, my Auntie Annie and Uncle George Clifford – largely, I think, by the persuasion of my cousin Laura (who I believe had a soft spot for me) – invited me to stay with them until something turned up. I have ever since been extremely grateful to the Clifford family for their kindness to me at that time.

While I was with them an advertisement appeared in one of the local papers to the effect that a certain building society was extending its operations to the Midlands and required four district superintendents who would work from an office in Birmingham. As a bond of faith the successful applicants would be required to put up £100 capital. Uncle George offered to put up the money to enable me to get this responsible position. I wrote for details, and the managing director, a Mr Caudle, came to my uncle's house to discuss the matter. Apparently he had already appointed three people – a man named Gem, with whom I was to work until I became *au fait* with the firm's methods, and two others whom I never saw. As things were a little vague and there was no Birmingham office we agreed to put down an advance payment of only £10 until the new office was open, which was to be done by a general manager living at Knighton in Herefordshire.

I made contact with Gem. He had been given a number of enquiries to follow up, which we did, but we could not clinch any business because we had not got an office with a bank account and all the necessary paperwork.

We were invited to dinner by one man who afterwards took us to the drawing room and plied us with whisky, wine and cigars. He said that he and we were all sharks living off a lot of simple idiots and we might as well work together and make a good job of it. His line was selling small retail businesses and ours was to finance the sales. He would put up the sales at prices well above their worth and we would provide money on easy payment terms which would be too attractive to refuse, but on which the clients would be certain to fall down and forfeit the businesses. We would split the profits. We said how attracted we were to the idea and got out of the place as quickly as possible!

After a couple of days we were having a drink in a pub when Gem said he was a bit concerned that no office had yet been opened in Birmingham. I asked him about the man at Knighton, and Gem said he had spent the whole of one day going from place to place with him in search of suitable offices and that he himself had paid for all the meals that day. I suggested that we get a list of office accommodation to let and request the Knighton man to come and fix it all up. This we did, and he turned up at New Street at the appointed time and we made a round of the offices, all of which he turned down. We broke off for lunch at a restaurant in Corporation Street and had a really good meal, at the end of which Gem and I got up by prior arrangement and left the other man with the bill. We waited outside till he came out in a rage demanding to know what we meant by such conduct, in reply to which we said that from the way he had turned down the office accommodation we had visited we were certain that he had not the slightest intention of opening any office. Whereupon he broke down and said he had no authority to open an office, that he had invested a sum of money in this concern and could not get any satisfaction from Caudle.

We then decided that we would ring the London headquarters address and it would cost us nothing if there was no reply. This we did and found that it was a disused number. At this, Gem and the Knighton man became really alarmed. Gem wrote to the last address Caudle had given him and received a reply from Bristol telling him there was nothing to worry about and would he go to Bristol where all would be made clear. I told him not to go till Caudle sent his fare, but he did go and I met him at New Street on his return. He reported that he had gone to the office address given and had seen Caudle alone in his office. He had apparently grabbed him by the lapels of his coat and demanded the immediate return of his money. At which Caudle told him not to be so daft and put over some explanation which had placated Gem – who, however, tried to assure me that he had frightened the life out of him. I told him he had done nothing of the sort but had made a complete mistake by seeing him without witnesses and alerting him to the fact that he had been rumbled.

I then wrote to Caudle indicating that I had the promise of business but that I should require an assurance of my expenses if I came to Bristol to explain it. He wrote back with that assurance and I went, but I arranged for my brother-in-law Mr Gay to meet me at the office and come in with me, but not say a word. (I hadn't had time to explain the position to him, I just wanted his presence to worry Caudle).

I had found out that the previous Tuesday Caudle had attended an examination in bankruptcy in London. We went upstairs to an office on the second floor, which was well furnished and, to my surprise, contained another superior gentleman, about thirty years old, to whom we were introduced, and I caught the title 'Captain'. Caudle asked about the business on offer and I said there were one of two points I wanted cleared up before we discussed that. I then said, 'What was the purpose of your visit to London on Tuesday last?', at which the Captain interrupted to ask what business that was of mine. In reply I asked him if he knew why Caudle went to London on that date, and anyway what exactly was his interest in what I had come about. He said if I was going to be aggressively impudent the interview would be ended. Whereupon I countered with the remark that in that case I would see that within a very short time of my leaving the office they would both be arrested.

This obviously startled both of them. The Captain became worried and angry, and Caudle became defiant. The Captain said there was nothing he could be arrested for and demanded an explanation. Referring to Mr Gay, who had said nothing but was quietly sitting, listening, Caudle said:

'No matter what your legal friend thinks my business in London was perfectly normal and legal and had nothing to do with this company or Captain –.'

This puzzled me, so I asked, 'What is the name of this company?'

I can't remember what name he gave, but it wasn't the name of the firm I was supposed to be employed by. The Captain said he was the chairman of this company, which had recently been formed to finance building mortgages and that Caudle was the secretary. I then realised that Caudle had fooled him. I asked a few more questions about the company and explained to the Captain, who was obviously honest, that the matter I had come to see Caudle about was connected with a totally different company. Caudle said he was sorry I had been inconvenienced but there was obviously a misunderstanding. The new company wanted men like me. Why didn't I join them as supervisor for the Birmingham area? I pretended to be attracted to this offer, and said I would probably accept and let them know, but as an earnest of good faith would he repay the deposit I had put down and my expenses to date. Caudle consulted the Captain who, on learning it was about £15, agreed to my being paid a cheque there and then, which they both signed. We all shook hands and we departed with expressions of goodwill, but needless to say I had not the slightest intention of further association with Caudle. I explained the position to Mr Gay, to whom I was very grateful, and returned to Birmingham.

We got the cheque into Uncle George's bank as soon as possible. It was drawn on a bank in the Forest of Dean – Lydney, I believe – and it was returned by that bank (as I feared it would be) with the curious endorsement 'Please resubmit'. We did this and were relieved to learn that it had been met! (I must remind you that while £15 does not seem to be much today it was a large sum of money at the time.) I did not expect to hear from Caudle again, but I read in a newspaper report sometime later that he had been jailed for fraud. Apparently during a service in a non-conformist church in Clevedon he had suddenly got up and announced that he had just had a call from God telling him to found a mission, and he took a collection there and then, but what happened afterwards I do not know. A report of his career of fraud appeared in the popular weekly journal, *John Bull*. I was sorry to learn from that report that Mr Gem had lost his investment.

Eight

A Guest in Gwaun-cae-Gurwen

Let not Ambition mock their useful toil,
Their homely joys, and destiny obscure;
Nor Grandeur hear, with a disdainful smile
The short and simple annals of the Poor.

(Thomas Gray, *Elegy Written in a Country Churchyard*)

After three or four weeks living with my aunt and uncle, all attempts to find work had come to nothing. I had to appeal to my sister Alice, asking whether she could provide me with living accommodation if I could pay my way by going on the dole. I was extremely grateful when Alice agreed to take me in.

I related earlier how David Merretti had come back from America and married Alice. Before he went away he had been an apprentice at the Gloucester Wagon Works, and as that was really his trade he tried to get suitable work in this field on his return. He obtained one or two jobs in Cheltenham but they were unsatisfactory. At last he took up an opportunity offered by Wagon Repairs Ltd, repairing coal wagons at their depot at the East Pit in Gwaun-cae-Gurwen in the west Wales anthracite district. He, Alice and Frank set up home in a council house at 17, Abernant Road, Cwmgorse, about two miles from the East Pit. The depot served six or seven pits (three of which became nationally notorious after the Second World War) and only had a small staff, of which Dave soon became foreman, so that the family were able to live very comfortably, though Dave was disliked by the Welsh workers and neither of them was very popular with the local people. However, I was very comfortable there.

I duly presented myself at the nearest Labour Exchange, which was one of about twenty lock-up shops, only half of which were occupied, which formed a pretty dismal covered arcade leading from the main street in Garnant to an open sort of no-man's-land completely bare of vegetation on the bank of the river Amman. Garnant was a small, typical tinplate town in the Amman valley, a couple of miles from Gwaun-cae-Gurwen. The Amman valley, with Ammanford as the main town, was very densely populated and was the centre of the Welsh anthracite coalfield.

The manager of the Exchange took down all my personal details and said, 'We don't often get people with your qualifications on our books, but I understand your position fully, and I might have the opportunity to compare notes sometime.' There did not seem to be many signing on, and during the next two or three weeks I was among very few unemployed, but then came a national strike on the railways which put all the pits out of work because the coal could not be shifted. The significance of this had not occurred to me until one day, arriving to sign on, I found a huge queue from the arcade all along the street of miners who had just come off the shift and, all covered in coal dust, were waiting to sign on too. I had to take my place in this queue and creep along to the Labour Exchange. When I got there I found that a trestle table had been wedged across the doorway and the manager, with a couple of other men, was frantically entering up names and details in unemployment books. As soon as I appeared the manager bawled out, 'Come on in, I've been waiting for you.' I said, 'How do I get in?'

'Over the table', he said, so I scrambled on to the top of the table and he dragged me over. Somehow or other I found myself sat down with a pile of books in front of me and an indelible pencil. It was all a terrible squeeze. He told me what questions to ask, then said, 'Get going. You've got yourself a job.'

And that's how I was restored to the ranks of normal civilised men, but it took me several days to get rid of the depression, the inferiority complex and the sense of hopelessness and slight shame from which I had been suffering while on the dole.

I forget how long the strike lasted, but while it was on we were dealing with several thousand miners. As this meant thousands of forms with details of dependants and so on, we were grossly overworked. I understood that we set up an all-time record for the number of people dealt with by each clerk. In spite of frantic appeals to Llanelli and Swansea, only one extra clerk could be obtained, as all the south Wales offices were overwhelmed. His name was Lloyd and he came up from Llanelli every day by bus. So the staff consisted of Rees the manager, supported by Lloyd and three temporary clerks – a mining engineer (temporarily unemployed), Jeffreys (the son of the retired butcher who lived next door to us and was our landlord) and myself.

We did an enormous amount of overtime, starting from the first day, on which I got home at about 8.30 p.m. to report to my very worried sister Alice what had happened. Each day we wedged the trestle table across the entrance, but it was no good, for by the time the office closed we had been pushed to the back wall by the pressure of men who for the first few days had come to register straight from the pits with loose coal dust on their clothes. What with that and the dust off the indelible pencils we used, which dyed our shirts through the V opening in our waistcoats and shaded our shirt sleeves upwards from a deep mauve at the cuffs, we needed a considerable clean-up when we got home. Fortunately the pay was good, and with the overtime we did very well financially, though I am sorry to say this did not apply to Mr Rees, who rather ruefully remarked to me one day that I was getting far more money than he was as he did not benefit from any overtime.

He was under contract to the Ministry of Labour by which he was paid £4 a week to run a Labour Exchange in Garnant in an office which he would provide and furnish. By then I knew he was a Bachelor of Commerce of Liverpool University and I expressed astonishment at this information for, although £4 a week was a fairly good basic wage, I did not see how it could be sufficient to maintain an office as well. He said he would explain some time, which he did one day after the strike was over and he had persuaded the authorities to allow me to stay on for two or three weeks to clear up the aftermath. He invited me to his home one evening. I was greatly impressed by his wife (who also had a degree from Liverpool University) and the taste and culture in his style of living. I confessed to being puzzled as to how to reconcile this with an overall income of £4 per week, so he explained that he was a native of Garnant who, after a due service in the Army, went to Liverpool University, where he met and married his wife. They both obtained degrees but could get no employment. Things became so desperate that he decided to come back to Garnant where he had, at least, some friends. So they decided to part for the time being. His wife returned to her parents in north Wales and he was to come back to Garnant, but he had no money at all to pay his fare or to buy food. So he decided to walk and beg for food on the way. And that's what he did. He arrived in Garnant practically all-in and the soles of his shoes nearly gone. He went to the manager of the Raven Tinplate Works, who had been a friend of the Rees family, and begged for some sort of work. The manager said the only job he could provide was one which called for considerable physical strength – a very heavy labouring job, that of a shearman trimming the rough edges of blocks of sheet steel, but the pay was good. Rees accepted, but as he was in bad physical shape the first few days nearly killed him (though when fit he had been the heavyweight boxing champion of the university). However, with good food he improved and by savage and sustained effort he reached a point where he was earning over £16 a week. He continued with this job until he had set up a home again, brought his wife down to Garnant and built up a reserve. He then saw the advert for a Labour Exchange manager and took the job, in spite of the drop in income, as it had many compensations which could not be measured in money, and provided him with the first step on the right ladder. He remarked cynically that 'as a labourer nobody wanted to know me, as the manager of the Labour Exchange everybody did.' My evening with him was unforgettable, especially as he gave a piano performance which was quite exceptional for an amateur.

I am immensely grateful to Mr Rees for the help he gave me just when I wanted it most. I do hope the future brought him compensation for the efforts he had to put out to get established. Somebody did tell me that about a year after the events I have described he was made manager of a large Exchange in north Wales.

Before I close the report on the Garnant episode there are two events which I think worth recording. One was an occasion when a miner in a big crowd in front of the wedged table started shouting at Rees in Welsh. Rees told him to shut up. He did not, so Rees stood up, reached across the table, caught hold of the front of the miner's shirt, pulled him forward and with all his strength hit him straight in the face, making blood spurt in all directions. The man fell backwards as if pole-axed. Rees jumped over the table into the crowd and shouted at them to get into line, which they did like sheep. I have never seen men so cowed. It was an object lesson in what an angry (but admittedly pretty big) man can do when confronted by a dangerous crowd.

The other incident concerns Jeffreys, the son of the retired butcher who owned our office. At the entrance to our arcade was the Star Supply Stores which opened on to the main street. The arcade, as I have already said, sloped down to an open sort of yard, and in this yard was the entrance to the portion of the building occupied by the Jeffreys family.

Apparently, about a couple of years previously the manager of the Star Supply Stores (who was a cripple) had been cashing up one Saturday night when he was stabbed to death with a carving knife, having been gagged with a lump of cheese. On the following Sunday morning, a lady teacher lodging with the Jeffreys, returning from early Communion, noticed that the light was still on in the stores, as could be seen through the back window overlooking the yard. Old man Jeffreys investigated and reported the murder; Scotland Yard was called in and the case was reported in the London papers. The knife was found under a heap of stones in the yard, and the experts said the murder was committed by a butcher or surgeon. Both Jeffrey senior and Jeffrey junior were strongly suspected and interviewed repeatedly over several months, but the elder Jeffrey had an alibi and the younger Jeffrey (our temporary clerk) put up a defence that he was so drunk that he had no recollection of anything but visiting the pub that evening. The defence seems pretty thin, but apparently they got away with it.

I was told all this one morning before Jeffrey arrived, and though I was interested I did not think much about it until one evening, when there was to be overtime, young Jeffreys asked me if I would go in with him to tea. I then thought about it quite a lot, for, entering by the yard door, I went into a darkish room from which stairs went up into the gloom, and was sniffed over by a black retriever dog. Old Jeffrey was a bloated, red-faced individual whom I would have thought capable of anything, and had a handshake like a wet cod. Mrs Jeffrey was a grey wispy sort of a person. The tea was alright but included rice pudding.

Some days later, on arrival at the office, the mining engineer said, 'You remember me telling you about that murder at the Star Supply Stores? Well this is the anniversary of that event.' Jeffreys arrived and the day passed till tea time when Jeffreys asked Lloyd if he would go in with him to tea. Lloyd went, and some time later rushed into the office where I was having a cup of tea with Rees. He said something terrible had happened and asked Rees to go with him. When they came back Rees reported that in the middle of tea old man Jeffrey, who had been looking at the newspaper, suddenly stood up, tried to say something, gurgled and collapsed right among the tea things. He never recovered.

The next morning the mining engineer on my arrival showed me a notice inserted in the 'In memoriam' column of a local daily paper. It had been inserted by the relations of the murdered manager of the Star Supply Stores. It said, 'Vengeance is mine, saith the Lord. I will repay.' An inquiry later in the day confirmed that this was the paper and the very page that old man Jeffrey had been reading.

The day came when Mr Rees had to say he could not persuade the Ministry to continue to employ me as a temporary clerk. So I had to resume my search for a permanent job, and the prospects looked dim, but to my surprise, in reply to a small ad in the *Western Mail*, a builder at Bridgend asked me to call and see him, which I did. The office was on a building site at Brynteg. It had been privately owned by a firm of Leicester building contractors who had been engaged on some large municipal undertakings near Swansea, but that work was finished and they did not wish to continue in south Wales. The Brynteg estate had been taken over by their general foreman, named Tickner, and the joinery foreman, called Hall, under the partnership name of Clarke and Tickner.

Actually I had to find Tickner out on the job, and when I had introduced myself he led me back to the office with hardly a word. It was a small wooden affair, furnished with a table and a couple of chairs set in the midst of chaos. Having got there, he said, 'Well this is the office. Can you take charge of it?' I was a bit nonplussed by my reception and frankly didn't know what to say, so I said, 'Yes', as I was desperate for the job, but I explained that I must be given some idea of what the firm did, how many employees they had, what were their wages and roughly what I was supposed to do. He explained a bit about the firm and gave me the wages book and the other account books to examine.

I said, 'It looks to me as if you want someone to relieve you of all the office work.' He said, 'That's it.' So I said, 'OK. You'll have to make allowances and answer a lot of questions but I'll do my best. When do I start?' He said, 'Now.' So, having agreed on a wage of £3/10 0 a week (which was quite good then) I started there and then to sort it all out. My sister Alice was surprised that I had not returned earlier but was, of course, delighted when I explained what had happened.

I obtained lodgings in Bridgend with a lady who proved to be stone deaf and somewhat mean. I had a sitting room and a bedroom, and another sitting room and bedroom were occupied by the Ministry of Agriculture's representative and adviser for south Wales. We all got on very well but both the Ministry of Agriculture man and myself were at the mercy of the landlady, who if she thought we were staying up late would simply walk in and turn off the gas light. She could not hear our protests, and there was nothing we could do but obey.

While there I entertained Mr Herbert Constance, who had taken over the management of the saw mills at Longhope. He was visiting Bridgend because that year it was the venue for the Royal Welsh Agricultural Show and Constance's were exhibiting their wooden turnery and other products for the first time. They won all the gold medals and first prizes it was possible to win in all the classes they entered.

Every Saturday I went by train and bus through Neath and Pontardawe to Cwmgorse and returned on Monday morning. This enabled me to participate in the social life there, and enjoy the whist drives organised by the church, of which Alice and Dave were leading members. Though, as I have said earlier, Alice and Dave were not generally popular they had some very good friends. Mr Hicks was head of the office at the famous Maerdy Pit which was owned by the Amalgamated Anthracite Co., and which operated the Peacock Vein of probably the best anthracite in the world. He was married to a particularly intelligent and vivacious Scotswoman, who became a great friend of Alice. But the most interesting personality was David Rees, a bachelor of about thirty years old. He was head of the office at the Cwmgorse Pit. He later became company secretary of the Amalgamated Anthracite Group, of which Lord Melchett was chairman, and he was secretary of the St David's Society, which was worldwide. Alice seemed to have an uncanny attraction for him (which I do not believe was sexual) and he spent practically every Sunday afternoon and evening with the Merretti family. This, and the fact that he was a member of the Church of Wales, was greatly resented by his mother, who was extremely Welsh and narrow-minded.

It is interesting to note that neither Frank Hall (Alice's son by Harry Hall) nor Michael Merretti (Alice's son by David) was taught English or taught in English for the first few years at school, by order of the Carmarthen Education Authority, although they were English. This proved to be a great handicap to them and to the Welsh pupils of the same age.

Just to illustrate how extraordinarily wealthy that corner of the country was at the time I think I should mention that the First Rollerman in the tinplate works was paid about £12 to £15 a week, while skilled engineers elsewhere were getting from £3 to £5. The coal that was dug in the Amman Valley was fetching the highest prices in the world and the Cwmgorse Pit was worth more than a gold mine to the owners, for every ounce of land yielded a return. The top soil was fertile and grew barley right up to the edge of the pit, which was a drift or 'level' mine which worked an outcrop of coal and followed the seam as the coal was extracted. Removal of the top soil laid bare a subsoil of clay, which was made into bricks. As this was removed and loaded on to vehicles the coal seam was exposed.

At one of the dances I was introduced to a very attractive and vivacious young lady named Regina Jones. She was the sister of the chief electrician at the East Pit (where Dave operated his wagon repairing) and a teacher at Cwmgorse School. Our acquaintance developed into a close friendship in which she visited Alice's frequently and I visited her home. We did not actually become engaged, but we undoubtedly would have, and been married, if I had settled permanently in Gwaun-cae-Gurwen. Fate, however, was to ordain otherwise.

Life continued like this for some months. I liked Bridgend, I liked my work. I was reasonably paid, and I was given a free hand in conducting the office work.

The Brynteg Estate where we operated was for private houses, built to about three different standard designs and specifications. Tickner lived in a temporary wooden house, as did Hall, the joiner partner, but they were building a pair of semi-detached houses for themselves, to one of the standard specifications, in their spare time. It is interesting to note that Tickner (an expert bricklayer) and Hall, with two men acting as labourers, built at a rate nearly twice as fast as an average of six men did constructing an identical pair of houses in normal working hours. The Building Trade Union laid down a maximum rate of 360 bricks in eight hours. Tickner could lay 100 bricks an hour with ease.

Just as I was beginning to think 'everything in the garden was lovely', the bricklayers decided to strike. After a couple of weeks Tickner came to me and said that, as no money was coming in, he was very sorry but he could not afford to keep me on. I was terror-struck at the prospect of being unemployed again and asked if he would continue my employment at half wages. After a little consideration he agreed to this, but there was no written regulation that office staff not party to a dispute must be kept on, and I felt I could not risk this again. So I decided to seek more certain employment, if possible in my own line and preferably in England.

The strike ended and operations were resumed, but I was looking out for a change of job. This came with an advert in the *South Wales Echo* from a firm requiring an assistant to the managing director at Highbridge in Somerset. This firm had bought a plant equipped for making ovoid fuel, and proposed to make these of anthracite duff which could be purchased for about eight shillings a ton plus freight from Swansea to Highbridge. Ovoid fuel had never been successfully made with anthracite until the introduction of a formula by a Mr T.A. Goskar, an engineer of Swansea who was managing director and works director of this new company, with his son as works chemist. The name of the firm was to be Highbridge Anthracite Fuels Ltd and I was to take charge of the office at a considerably increased salary. I signed a year's contract and agreed to start within a month of notice that operations were to commence.

But in the meantime something happened which, if it had occurred before, might have made the change unnecessary and altered the whole course of my life.

As you will have gathered, our office was quite small and Tickner and I sat alongside one another at a long desk under the window. We were at such close quarters that when he was interviewing a client or visitor I could hear every word. Well one day a visitor called who said he was the South Wales Representative for the British Imperial Cable Company and he was authorised to order a house to live in. This was to contain an office and to be of a superior specification so that he could entertain important clients. He looked through our standard designs and turned them all down as quite unsuitable. Tickner could offer nothing more so the man got up to go. Now I thought it would be a tragedy to miss such a good order so I interrupted the conversation and asked the said gentleman if he could give me some idea of what he had in mind, stating the features he regarded as essential and the maximum price he would pay. He sat down again and did this, at the end of which I said if he would call the following afternoon we might have something acceptable to show him. He agreed and departed. When he had gone Tickner asked what I meant by my offer and how could we possibly have anything to show him the next day. I said I would get out some rough drawings by the time stated.

I worked all night and the next morning. He called in the afternoon. We presented the drawings and discussed the specification and price. He placed a provisional order subject to confirmation and approval of final drawings and specification. I produced these in a few days, and the contract was signed. The plans were accepted by Bridgend District Council and building commenced. When it was finished our client was very pleased.

Tickner was delighted, though he did not show it. In fact, though we got on well, he seldom showed an emotion of any sort and was a man of very few words. However, this incident opened up new vistas for him. He expressed the greatest surprise at my efforts. 'Gosh', he said, 'If you can design and draw houses like that, we can really go to town', and whenever a customer wanted something different from our standard houses I produced something to his liking within days. On one occasion I even put through two houses in one week.

This did not last long, for I received from Highbridge Fuels the date I was to start. I had to give a month's notice and was making up my mind to do this, when Tickner sat alongside me at the desk one day and started talking of our rosy future, saying 'We'll do this', and 'We'll do that.' The more he romanced, the more embarrassed I became until at last I said, 'Who is this *we* you keep talking about?', and the astonishing reply came, 'Us – you and me.' I was perplexed but managed to say, 'I'm afraid you will have to forget all that. There can't be any future for you and me', and I explained the position and formally gave in my notice.

Tickner sat there for a while and said nothing, then went out and did not come back that day. Nor the next, but his wife came and said that he was very upset. She begged me to stay and said they would like me to accept a partnership in the business.

I asked for time to consider it but decided to refuse, partly because I had accepted a contract with another firm and partly because I really did not wish to spend the rest of my life in Wales. I had been very happy there and made many friends. There was a lot I liked and admired about Wales and the Welsh, but I wanted to get back, if possible, to Gloucestershire, and I did not wish to impose myself on Alice and Dave any longer than I could help.

The parting with Tickner's made me very uncomfortable. They said I could go back at any time, and I would be welcome to stay with them if I was ever in that part of the country again, but I never went back, as I do not believe in it. I wonder what happened to them all.

'Springtime' (above) and 'Harvest' (below), painted by Arthur in the late 1920s, probably after he moved back to Gloucestershire.

Nine

Factory Stacks

And the lovely Laughing Water
Seemed more lovely, as she stood there,
Neither willing nor reluctant,
As she went to Hiawatha,
Softly took the seat beside him,
While she said, and blushed to say it,
'I will follow you, my husband'.

(H.W. Longfellow, *The Song of Hiawatha*)

Sometime in 1925 I took up residence as a lodger with Mrs Knight in a terraced street parallel with, and immediately behind, the sea front at Burnham-on-Sea, about two miles from the factory at Highbridge. I ran the office with the assistance of two young ladies, a clerk and a secretary.

The ships bringing the anthracite duff from Swansea discharged their cargoes direct to the factory from a quay right opposite, and the production of ovoids commenced. We registered the name 'Glovoids', and they were highly efficient. They had the characteristics of anthracite – that is, they gave intense local heat with a higher calorific value than bituminous ovoids – but they did not naturally coke and they tended to become friable and disintegrate so that there was an appreciable loss when the trucks were roughly shunted. This was a distinct disadvantage, especially as people were not used to them and they had to be sold at a very competitive price to attract custom against all the other different sorts of fuel. It was very difficult to establish a market, and the firm (which was owned by some financiers in London and the proprietors of the 'Veda' patent bread in Edinburgh) was undercapitalised, with the result that operations only lasted about eighteen months. They would have lasted longer but for the fact that Goskar, being a technical man rather than a business man, started experimenting to produce a smokeless ovoid. Having used the normal matrix (pitch) to bind the duff into an ovoid, he found he had also made the fuel smoky. The only way to remove the smoke was to coke the fuel; but anthracite will not coke, so the coking process merely meant that we burnt out the pitch that had been used to bind the dust particles together – a futile exercise.

I got on with everyone very well. Goskar was amiable, if somewhat unpractical. My digs were comfortable, and on the whole I enjoyed my stay at the seaside, but I was, of course, very disappointed that the enterprise had proved a failure and that I again

The Ramping Cat between Cam and Dursley is now a private dwelling, but still bears its unusual sign and is remembered as a pub by locals.

had to seek employment. I wrote to my sister Lucy to ask if she could put me up until I could make other arrangements. She agreed, and at the end of 1926, somewhat dejected, I went to stay with mother and Lucy at Cromwell Road, Bristol.

On my arrival I looked through the *Western Daily Press* to see if anybody wanted my services and found there was a vacancy in the office of an engineering firm in Gloucestershire. I wrote an application and posted it that afternoon. A few days later I had a letter from R.A. Lister & Co. Ltd of Dursley, inviting me to an interview at the Bristol office of Greenslades, bellows manufacturers. There I met Mr Percy Lister (later Sir Percy), and he engaged me as a clerk to work in the general office at Dursley, to commence on 1 January 1926. I was then twenty-six years old.

Dursley welcomed me with several inches of snow. I was installed as an invoice clerk in the Forwarding Office. For a short while I lodged in the home of the district nurse, where I was very comfortable. Staying there was a Queen's nurse from Glasgow, attracted south by railway posters showing how sunny, warm and generally delightful the south of England is in midwinter! One evening when I got in she had just returned from a train-cum-bus trip to the Cheddar Gorge. Although it was snowing and she was the only person there, she had walked right up the gorge. She said it was eerie to the point of being frightening, and recommended it for anyone seeking a new experience. I don't expect she ever came south again in midwinter.

It was not long before I moved to the garden suburb, where I had a bedroom and shared a sitting room with a Mr William (Bill) West, mathematics master at the

The Priory, Dursley, in 1927.

Dursley mixed secondary school. He later became the best man at my wedding. I shall always remember my first Sunday there. Snow was still thick on the ground, and West suggested a walk. Half an hour later found us discussing everything under the sun in a small pub in Upper Cam, just below the Dursley gasworks. This pub was named the New Inn but was always referred to as the Ramping Cat. In that walk and conversation I found out that Mr West was a somewhat disillusioned romantic idealist, one time Methodist local preacher who had become a cynical socialist atheist, naive enough to believe in the possibility of a state in which all men and women were equal and everyone was kind, loving and altruistic. Though highly intelligent, he laughingly denied all knowledge of geography, while insisting on the correctness of his assessment of world affairs, which, without geography, could have no basis. I give this analysis of his character because he illustrates the trend which was creeping into our universities and schools at the time, a mixture of anarchy, socialism, atheism, cynicism, permissiveness and general unreality which later resulted in the breakdown of social discipline and organised society.

I lived with Bill West for some time and enjoyed his company in spite of my dislike of his opinions. He eventually married a young lady teacher, his childhood sweetheart, who was a much stronger character than he was, so I expect everything worked out all right.

Lister's manufactured petrol engines, electric lighting plants, cream separators, butter churns, a whole range of dairy utensils, sheep-shearing machinery, ornamental tubs and garden furniture – a twenty-four-hour-a-day operation. Their products were exported all over the world, as well as being supplied to 6,000 retailers in the United Kingdom.

The Priory, Dursley, still the headquarters of Lister Petter.

In 1927 the number of employees was probably just under 2,000, but this number was greatly increased during the period of my employment, as was the range and quantity of goods made. Details will be found in the book I later wrote on behalf of the firm, entitled *Your Works and Ours*, setting out Lister's history and achievements.

The head office was in a very old and interesting house known as the Priory, built in 1520. It had been the home of Sir Ashton Lister, the founder of the business, until he moved to a new, larger house called the Towers, built on the hillside above the works.

There were about twenty-five people in the Forwarding Office. The male clerks roughed out the invoices and the girls typed them, after which they were scrupu-

The Forwarding Office at R.A. Lister & Co., where Arthur worked in the late 1920s.

lously checked by a Mr Robins. There was not much time for fooling around, and anyone who did was promptly sacked. (Trade Unions were not officially recognised.) But although discipline was strict, as elsewhere in the firm, and although we were fully employed, it was a happy place.

While working there I looked round once or twice at the entry of a young lady who had come to consult Mr Robins about something. She always seemed to be framed in the doorway. She had dark brown hair and eyes with a very pretty round face, was slim and of medium height, and her favourite dress seemed to be a frock with a green-blue Paisley-patterned top and a navy blue serge skirt. I found her very attractive, and on enquiring to a fellow clerk who she was I was told to keep my eyes off her, as she was the private secretary of the managing director, Mr Percy Lister.

It wasn't very long before I was moved to the Accounts Department, which was housed in what had been a large and somewhat ornate greenhouse built on the side of the main house adjacent to, and entered from, the Forwarding Office on the one side and the garden on the other. The boss was a Mr Ted Snow (landlord of the Castle Inn), with Bill Wyatt as deputy and a staff of several clerks and typists.

Both Snow and Wyatt were very witty, and Snow could bring the house down at will, with his 'take-offs' of Gill, the company secretary and accountant (to whom he was responsible). Snow, who was getting on towards retirement, did not do much work, and one day Bill Wyatt accidentally came across bills of exchange worth £4,000 (probably nearer £400,000 in 2009) stuffed down behind a cupboard. These bills should have been sent months before to Australia for payment. Bill Wyatt was in a

Lister's Tennis Club, of which Arthur was secretary, in 1926. Arthur is in the back row wearing a suit and tie; his future wife, Vera, is seated on the ground to the left of the little boy. The grass tennis court is now a bowling green and looks much the same.

dilemma. He did not want to hurt Snow but was bound to report it. I never learnt the outcome, but not long afterwards Snow disappeared and we heard he had retired.

Some while subsequent to this I was placed in charge of the sales office of the ornamental tub and garden furniture department. This department had evolved as an offshoot of the churn works to salvage and turn into money the shaped oak staves which cracked while being coopered into churn tubs; also to keep down the overheads of the saw mills in which the wooden packing cases were made for other lines. Supplemented by ornamental bellows, made by Greenslades of Bristol and carved with scenes from Burns and Dickens, these lines grew into big business and were found in some of the finest hotels and on the biggest luxury liners in the world.

For this job I was given a separate office and secretary, plus about a dozen travelling salesmen. Four of these were in London, and one day I needed to replace one of them. We had a poor response to our advertisement, but one applicant presented himself in person. There was considerable unemployment at the time, and he was determined to get the job. His suit had an old-fashioned cut and he wore a bowler hat. He came from Glasgow, spoke in the broadest Scots and was an ex-steeplejack. As he would have to call on the big fashionable stores in London, where, incidentally, he had never been, and had no selling experience, he seemed a hopeless prospect, but he begged to be taken on and would not take no for an answer. He had no money and only the clothes he stood up in. Remembering my own experience and in view of his earnestness, I agreed to employ him, and I got the cashier (Herbie Harris) to advance sufficient money to fund him for a month. He left on the train for London

Arthur's wife, Frances Vera (née Wyatt), who worked as Sir Percy Lister's personal assistant. She was named Frances after her mother, yet was always known as Vera.

with all the necessary paperwork that same day, and I sent up a silent prayer that I was not going to be proved a fool. I heard nothing for a week or two and then orders began to come in. During the next six months he outsold the other three salesmen put together. He was still going when I left the department, but I heard later that he left for a much better job.

I must now refer again to the young lady who made visits to the Forwarding Office. I found out that her name was Vera Wyatt (no relation to Bill), and sometimes I happened to be walking up Long Street either at midday or after work at the same time as she was, so naturally we got into conversation, and before I knew where I was I found myself sitting in the Victoria Cinema in the next chair or walking alongside her on Cam Peak. Introductions to her parents followed, together with visits to their home, Lynwood, in the Everlands Path at Cam.

Now my landlady at Burnham, Mrs Knight, who was a dedicated reader of fortunes in teacups, had one day before I left and so read a teacup of mine. 'Ah', she had said, 'One thing is certain about the place that you are going to shortly. You will notice that there are two tall factory stacks close to one another, and they will have some bearing on your life.'

It was not long after I commenced visiting Lynwood that I noticed two factory stacks a little farther along the Everlands Path towards Cam. They belonged to a famous woollen factory called Cam Mills, many of whose personnel later became great friends of mine.

Lynwood, Everlands, Cam, was designed and built for Vera's parents, Frederick and Frances Wyatt. They were allegedly upset when some people down the road employed the builder to construct an almost identical house! It has changed little since the 1930s, as can be seen when compared to the picture on page 144.

Vera's home, Lynwood, as it looked in the 1930s. It has changed very little, except for the loss of the standard roses and part of the lawn to make way for the inevitable parking spaces. Frederick Wyatt was a driver of the steam trains that served the branch line to Dursley.

My visits to Lynwood became more frequent and I came to know and like Vera's sister, Elsie, and her two brothers, Wilf and Den. We went away together on holiday to Evesham, where Vera once worked, and also to Torquay, where we had quite an adventure getting suitable accommodation one August Bank Holiday.

It was either punting on the river Avon at Evesham, where I got the seat of my white flannel trousers stained a deep red from a wet cushion, or at Torquay, that either she asked me to marry her or I asked her if she would marry me. We have never been able to decide which, but it is certain that whoever was asked immediately agreed, because on Saturday 1 September 1928 we were married in Rycroft Methodist Chapel at Gloucester, which Vera had attended as a child.[20] The wedding reception was at Sunnymede, Grafton Road, Gloucester, the home of Elsie and her husband Cyril Gibbs, a senior employee of the well-known auctioneers, Bruton Knowles of Gloucester.

We spent our honeymoon in Folkestone at the Langhorne Hotel, just above the Leas Cliff Pavilion. On the Sunday we visited a church at which the Revd Elliott, the first radio parson, was minister, and heard him preach from what was then the best-known pulpit in Britain. Then on Monday we went to see an England Eleven play the West Indies in the first match of the Kent Cricket Festival. I particularly wanted to see this as Woolley was playing for England and the famous West Indies fast bowler Constantine was playing for them. I was doubtful if this was going to meet with Vera's approval, but it was perfect weather, as it was all the week, and she enjoyed it.

We returned to our own new house, built in the Everlands Path on land acquired from Elsie and Cyril, two plots down from Lynwood. It had been designed by me and

Yartleton, Arthur and Vera's first marital home (above), was designed by Arthur and is situated on Everlands, a couple of plots further on from Vera's parents' home, Lynwood. Since the 1970s it has been extended and altered from its original state somewhat detrimentally (below), but the hollyhocks would have met with the approval of its original residents.

Arthur and Vera's wedding in 1928. Vera's outfit was of georgette fabric in the unusual colour combination of mauve and peach. The hat and its trim of flowers were made by her sister, Elsie, an expert milliner. Their daughter Nancy records with surprise that, rather than treasuring her wedding outfit, Vera later used it as household rags!

was named Yartleton after the real name of May Hill in west Gloucestershire. Heating and lighting was by gas, as electricity was not then available; nor was there a public water supply. Water was pumped up out of our own well, which had been located for us by Bill Wyatt who was an amateur water diviner. It was directly opposite and a couple of yards from the back door. I can't remember the cost of the house, but it must have been about £500 plus a subsidy, for we sold it years later, at a profit, for £750. It remained as built until 1978 when it was enlarged.

About 11 a.m. on Sunday 3 August 1930 I received a note from Nurse Smith, who ran the nursing home at Cam. The note said, '10.00 am. A little girl', and that little girl was Nancy. We were of course delighted, though Vera had had a bad time which necessitated a later operation. This limited the family to one, though the doctors had assured us it would not be so.

It has always been a matter of regret to me that my mother did not live long enough to see Nancy, but they passed one another, one on the way out and one the way in, since she died in Bristol Royal Infirmary on 22 February 1930, just over five months before Nancy's arrival. She had been living with my sister Lucy in Bristol. When we got the news that she was in the infirmary we went straight to Bristol to visit her but on arrival at the office were informed that she had died that morning and had been moved to the mortuary, where we placed a bunch of snowdrops we had brought. She looked very small and frail, but she had the heart of a lion.

A family group photograph outside Yartleton, Everlands, Cam, in the mid-1930s.
Back row:Vera Bullock with her parents, Frederick and Frances Wyatt. Middle:Arthur's sister
Lucy with her first husband, Mr Gay. Front: Nancy.

We were very happy living in Cam, which was a lively village with a vigorous Methodist community, a choral society and cricket, football and tennis clubs. There were two primary schools and two churches. Mr Wyatt was a steward of the chapel and all the family attended regularly and participated in all the many chapel activities.Vera and I were members of the choral society and the tennis club. As the result of all these connections, and the fact that we were on the staff of Lister's, we were known to everybody and most people were known to us. Our closest friends were the Underwood family. Mr Underwood was a chapel steward and home sales manager for Hunt and Winterbotham, who owned Cam Mills and who manufactured what was claimed to be the best worsted cloth on Earth.They had shops on the SS *Queen Mary*, the SS *Queen Elizabeth*, in Bond Street, London, and on Fifth Avenue, New York. Edith Underwood was Vera's closest friend for many years, Jessie Underwood married Vera's brother Dennis, and there was one other daughter named Constance.

The Cam Choral Society, conducted by the wife of the schoolmaster at Cam Hopton School, was a prize winner at the Stinchcombe Hill Musical Festival and at the Cheltenham Musical Festival. At one of the concerts which wound up the Stinchcombe Hill Festival, which was being conduced by Dr Darke, organist at Westminster Abbey, the front row of the audience was composed of Dr Vaughan Williams, Imogen Holst (daughter of Gustav Holst), the composer and conductor Herbert Howells, the poet laureate John Masefield, and the portrait painter Sir William Rothenstein.

Vera, Nancy and Arthur Bullock in the mid-1930s.

As it happens, Vera and I were largely responsible for the formation of a rival choral society in Cam, which was called the Cam Village Choir. Both choirs competed in the same Cheltenham Festival one year. Our choir won the chief trophy – the Choral Cup – and Cam Choral Society was second. In doing so, we both beat big choirs from the Midlands and south Wales, one being Cardiff Orpheus Society with ninety-two members. The adjudicator was Sir Granville Bantock, who was so astonished that he asked where the Cam choirs came from: 'Was it Cambridge?' On being informed that they both came from the same village in Gloucestershire he was flabbergasted and asked if there was anybody left in the village that afternoon. The report of this in the press led to a debate by readers' letters in the national newspapers as to which was the most musical village in England!

DIAMOND JUBILEE – 1927

The directors and office staff of R. A. Lister and Co., Dursley, Gloucestershire

Front row : S. Wooldridge, E. C. Hollingsworth, H. Pegler, P. Ashworth, F. Smith, A. Jones, H. Du Rose, W. Morgan, H. Wooldridge, J. T. Rymer, G. A. Lister, A. C. Lister, R. B. Lister, Sir Ashton Lister, H. Lister, A. E. Mellerup, Major C. Pratt, M. Cummings, A. F. Saunders, J. Seabourne, H. S. Robins, L. Dalby, H. H. Harris, B. H. Snell.

Frances Vera Wyatt stands directly behind her boss, C. P. (Percy) Lister. Her future husband, Arthur Stanley Bullock, is on the far left of the fourth row.

The directors and office staff of R. A. Lister & Co. in 1927. Robert Ashton Lister is in the front row holding a hat, flanked by his five sons. One place to the right, with his legs crossed, is Percy Lister. Behind him stands his PA, Vera Wyatt, later to marry Arthur (who is far left, fourth row back).

Ten

Life at Lister's

My mind to me a kingdom is,
Such present joys therein I find,
That it excels all other bliss
That worlds afford or grows by kind.
Though much I want which most would have,
Yet still my mind forbids to crave.

(Sir Edward Dyer)

There were five Lister brothers who were actively engaged in the business while I was there: Robert, the eldest; George, in charge of the home sales except industrial engines and lighting plants; Percy, who was managing director and foreign sales director; Frank, in charge of buying; and Cecil, who seemed to be assistant to everybody. All these were sons of Charles Lister, who lived in America under a cloud after being removed from the board. He had two brothers: Austin, who was nominal chairman of the company, and Stewart, who lived in Canada running his own business. Percy was by far the cleverest and most dominant director, and during all my remaining time there I was directly responsible to him.

While we traded in all lines all over the world, Australia and New Zealand accounted for the greatest share of our export business, including as it did farm engines, lighting plants, sheep-shearing machinery and cream separators. Much of Vera's work as Percy's private secretary was correspondence with the very substantial firms representing us in Australasia[21], and when she left I took over all correspondence relating to our trade in Asia and Australasia. As assistant to Percy Lister (and on my own in his absence) I handled all sales in that area, and later in Canada and Africa as well, right up to the termination of my employment there.

It was understood that this was my job, but as the years went by a number of other responsibilities were added to my workload. I felt honoured that I was selected to do this extra work, and as a result I became probably better informed as to the past history and current operations of the whole business than anybody else, including the directors. However, I received no financial reward – not one penny in addition to my basic salary of £4 per week.

I wrote occasional articles for the *Lister Standard*, a house magazine which went out to our main agents to inform them of developments and kept them interested

A Lister's employee demonstrating a cream separator.

The capstan lathe shop at Lister's, from a commemorative collection of photographs issued by the company in the late 1920s.

The Lister foundry in the late 1920s: (above) engines; (below) cream separators.

in the firm – a semi-sales, semi-public relations exercise. In addition, Percy Lister asked me to start *Lister News*, to interest employees in what the firm and their fellow employees were doing, and as a medium of special internal information. I was supposed to make it pay a profit and ensure that it appeared simultaneously in every part of the works and offices so that employees should not be tempted to borrow instead of buy. It was impossible to produce it within the conditions laid down and do my own job as well. Percy Lister was dismissive, so I just stopped producing it and said I would do one job or the other, but not both. He passed it to the advertising department, to be a much more elaborate publication produced by a small team. It cost so much that few bought it, so a considerable loss resulted and one issue was the end of that.

Another additional duty resulted from the many criticisms I received from over-seas agents about the quality of the instruction books for engines, separators and sheep-shearing machinery. When I complained of this to Percy Lister he told me to take control and act as editor and issued the necessary instructions to the advertising department. Similarly, when I criticised the layout and blurb of the engine catalogue the advertising department was instructed that I was to edit future issues. A folder advertising engines for export, entitled *From Greenland to Grigualand, From Piccadilly to Peru*, was produced under my direction, as was another folder advertising cream separators. I had my daughter Nancy photographed for the illustration of the young lady turning the handle, but she proved to be too small.

The efficiency bonus for employees not paid by results was a very good scheme which also greatly reduced the amount of scrap. It did not get going as quickly as was hoped, so one day Percy Lister said to me that he wanted me to sell the idea to the works. Apart from holding out a promise of more than the scheme could fulfil I could go anywhere and talk to whom I liked, but he wanted everyone to understand it and do everything possible to get the most out of it. So I tried to carry out his wishes and for a while results improved, but then 'the needle seemed to get stuck in the groove'. Trying to find the cause, I was referred again and again by the day workers to the piece workers who did not come into the scheme, though its success depended on their cooperation. They would not discuss it with me unless I guaranteed I would not mention their names to the directors. I gave this assurance, and I was informed that they would do no more than they were doing unless the existing rates were frozen for an agreed period for any particular job. I put this to Percy Lister. I refused to divulge any names, but pointed out that unless this was agreed to, the scheme had reached its limit, and I could do no more. He was sympathetic, but pointed out that his decision depended on his fellow directors and the Engineering Employers' Association, by whose rates Lister's had to abide. He promised me an answer in days. When it came it was to the effect that no such freezing of rates could be agreed to. So I asked to be relieved of the job, to which he agreed.

One of my proudest achievements while at Lister's was the creation of a permanent, always up-to-date reference book and price list for engine spare parts, for main agents, which enabled them to quickly identify the part required and order with certainty any spare part for any of the eighty different engines that we manufactured. It saved no end of correspondence and misunderstandings, and enabled agents to maintain stocks of spares for prompt and adequate servicing at a far lower cost than would otherwise have been possible. This was particularly welcomed by overseas agents (it was because of their difficulties that I had suggested it). Percy Lister approved it and told me to go ahead with 200 of the lists.

I had special hard loose-leaf covers made, strong enough to last for years, to take about 400 pages about 12in by 8in, which listed all the parts ever made by Lister's and all the engines in which each of those parts was used, with sufficient description for quick identification, cross-referenced in every possible way. Periodically a set of new sheets would be sent out to include all new introductions and advise as to parts made obsolete. These sheets would replace those made out of date, which were transferred to a sub-file.

One day Percy Lister said to me:

Keep this under your hat, but we have appointed a publicity agent to keep our name constantly before the public, outside the advertising pages. It has cost us a lot of money so we want to get the maximum out of it, and I want you to see that we do. This agency is run by Sidney Walton who controls a number of newspapers and magazines, is on various hospital and other boards, brags in *Who's Who* that he once refused a knighthood, and won a wager that he would sell a gramophone record to the King. He is a lay preacher, and despite a pleasant and benevolent demeanour he is as cynical and ruthless as they come. He has appointed a man named Lawrence to look after our affairs, so all contact between Walton and Lister's will be through yourself and Lawrence. Feed them well with suitable items and watch both of them. You will be receiving a lot of newspaper cuttings which will have to be filed for reference.

This was the beginning of a lot of stunt advertising through the news columns, including a nationwide broadcast of an offer by Lister's to boost exports by setting up an export promotion fund, in which Lister's would provide £1 for every £1 put up by the Government. I can't remember all the details but the impression was given that Lister's had gone all altruistic on a national scale. What a hope! The fact was that the figures were far beyond anything likely to be accepted, so there was no scheme, and Lister's got all that publicity for nothing. Phoney arguments about sheep-shearing records were set up in the correspondence columns of newspapers, most of the letters for and against being written by Lawrence.

At length Percy Lister said to me, 'I can't see why we have got to pay Walton for a lot of letters to the press that we could write ourselves. See what you can do to set up a correspondence exchange.'

So I did, but I can't remember what about. A few days later a letter came from Walton to Percy Lister which read something like this:

Dear Lister, Lawrence tells me that you have attempted to run your own publicity in the correspondence columns of the press. May I remind you that you are under contract to me for all press publicity. Don't waste your time writing any more letters to the papers. They will not be published.

Arthur was interested in economics in all its facets. The bills of exchange drawn on the HSBC (above) show that Lister's were doing business with the Far East on a large scale well before the Second World War. The Rentenmark note (below, nothing to do with Lister's) dates from the 1930s and was issued when hyperinflation caused the collapse of the German Mark.

Percy Lister did not take kindly to that sort of talk but he realised that he, like many others, was in Walton's clutches and could be blackmailed. He decided to get out. I don't know how he did or how much it cost him, but before that Walton did one more service. I was to edit a book which Percy Lister had asked me to compile and write. The book was called *Your Works and Ours*[22], and it was to contain a short history of the firm, a description of all its products and activities, and details of conditions of employment, pension schemes, medical facilities available to employees, social and recreational activities – in fact everything about the firm which any reasonable employee would want to know. The plan was to give one of these to every employee when engaged. It was an excellent idea and I often wondered if it was continued after the first edition was exhausted and I had left the firm.

Apart from getting the language dolled up a bit by some slick journalist on his staff, Walton contributed nothing to this and I was entirely responsible for its production and printing. But I'm afraid this brought me into conflict with some of the directors, in particular Percy's brother Robert. Although they accepted his dominance, not all that Percy did met with the approval of his brothers, and if they could drop a spanner in the works without being seen, they would do so. As I seemed to be the executive for a lot of his ideas, I experienced considerable difficulty in getting the cooperation of Robert, George and Frank, but particularly the first two, who were older than Percy and were jealous of him. In the front of the booklet are photographs of all the directors. I only got these after repeated application and I could not get Robert's photograph at all. He just would not let me have it, and it held up the publication. Percy kept asking when it would be printed, and I kept explaining. So at last I told the printers, Baileys, who published the *Dursley Gazette*, to go ahead and print, omitting Robert's photo, but to stop assembly and stapling after making up one copy. This they did, and I presented it to Percy Lister, pointing out that Robert's photo was missing.

He was furious with me, and wanted to know what I was playing at. I told him he had left me no option: he had demanded the booklet, but I could not force Robert to produce his photo. Percy took the sample and tore upstairs to Robert's office. What took place I do not know, but in days I had Robert's photo and the booklet was printed. But from that day I was a marked man.

Baileys did the printing of this and many other things for Lister's, including the *Lister News* and the *Lister Standard*, so I saw a lot of Fred Bailey, the proprietor. One day, discussing one of these publications, I happened to mention Sidney Walton. 'What do you know about Sidney Walton?' he asked. I told him I was not at liberty to tell him anything, but he said it was of great importance to him. So, binding him to the strictest confidence, I told him what I knew and what I thought. He thanked me and said, 'You have saved me from making a complete fool of myself. Sidney Walton has been trying to get control of the *Dursley Gazette* and had made me an offer which I can now see might have been disastrous.' I never learnt what was the outcome of all this, but I do know that Bailey's prospered and eventually purchased the *Stroud Journal*.

One day Percy Lister rang for me, and I found two men in his office, one of whom named Tombs he introduced as a film producer from New Zealand, whose company intended to put on a series of documentary films featuring English counties, starting with Gloucestershire. They intended also to offer one big company in each county the oppor-

Lister's works offices in Long Street, later destroyed by fire.

tunity of sponsoring the film and deriving as much advertising as possible from it without making it into an advertising film. Lister's had been chosen for this one. I was to write the scenario, to include the story of Gloucestershire ancient and modern – the latter to include its industries (particularly Lister's), a description of its scenery and its social life.

The second man was the freelance cameraman who was to take the film. He was introduced as Mr Hodgson and was one of the leading freelance cameramen in the country, having made a wonderful documentary on whaling for Lever Bros. Having written the scenario I was to take these two gentlemen to the various locations and try to ensure that what I had written down was translated into pictures.

This proved to be a story in itself and I would not have missed it for worlds. Hodgson's camera had taken him to nearly every country in the world and his extraordinary experiences kept us well entertained on our journey around. He was, however, the most awkward 'cuss'. So jealous was he of his reputation as a leading international cameraman, that he took a lot of persuading to take shots necessary to the story but which he did not think would enhance his reputation, and he refused point blank to take any picture in which there was nothing alive or moving, except the mosaic floors of the Roman Villa at Chedworth.

The film was a tremendous success in New Zealand and stole the limelight of the big pictures on the same programme. It was repeated three times in the main cities and appeared in practically every cinema in the dominion, where it was described in the advertisements as 'a camera jaunt through Gloucestershire in England's glorious springtime.' Actually it was shot between 14 October and 8 November and we raced from place to place, primarily to finish the filming before the last leaves had fallen and left the trees bare, and partly to get the filming done before the light faded each day.

The fact that this was really an advertising film in the guise of a documentary became a little awkward when we wanted to include one of England's most famous hunts – the Berkeley. Frank Lister, who was a leading member of this very exclusive hunt (based at Berkeley Castle) phoned Captain Berkeley to ask permission to take pictures of a meet of the hounds at the castle, for a New Zealand company wishing to make a documentary of English life. This was given provisionally, on condition that it was not in any way to be used for advertising, and a date was fixed.

Percy Lister warned me that under no circumstances were the hunt people to suspect the taint of advertising and said that at the interview I was to do all the talking. Sure enough, Captain Berkeley and the Master of Fox Hounds, Colonel somebody or other, had us into the office and cross-examined me unmercifully, but at last they were satisfied and cooperated in every way to enable us to get a splendid series of pictures. At that time the Berkeleys would allow no photographers to take any interiors of exteriors of the castle, so we did not ask them to break this rule. They would, however, have been surprised to learn that the aeroplane which swooped backwards and forwards just above the roof a few days after contained our friend Hodgson taking the most marvellous set of photos.

One reason why Gloucestershire was chosen as the first county to be filmed in this series was that the Governor General of New Zealand at that time was Viscount Bledisloe, who lived at Lydney Park in the Forest of Dean. He was to be invited to the premier showing in Wellington, and he must have been pleasantly surprised to find that the film opened with some lovely shots of his own home, with the deer drifting across the foreground and the Union Jack flying from the flagpole on the roof. I have said how popular it was in New Zealand, and should add that afterwards it went to Australia and finally landed up at the British trade exhibition in Johannesberg.

Before ending my remarks about this film there is something else I really must refer to.

Our film included quite a bit about Beverston Castle, near Tetbury, because Lister's resident representative for Australia and New Zealand for twenty-seven years was a man named Garlick (who was probably responsible for the sale of more sheep-shearing machinery than any other man). Garlick's family owned Beverston Castle, and he was born there. In the year 1336, as mentioned in the film, 5,000 Cotswold sheep were shorn in the castle courtyard. I wonder if this is a world record.

Garlick lived in Sydney. He never married but was a naturalist of some repute. He did a wonderful job for Lister's, and I liked him very much. He did not really like Australia and was longing for his retirement and return to the Cotswolds, but alas, flying one day from Melbourne to Hobart in Tasmania, he disappeared and was presumably drowned in the Bass Strait.

The death of Garlick left a vacancy which had to be filled, as he was by far the most important outside representative of the firm. As he was due to retire in two or three years his replacement had been discussed on a visit of Percy Lister to Australia. Garlick reported this to me in our private correspondence. He also reported that he had strongly urged that I should be appointed, but Percy Lister said this had been considered and turned down because I was not a good mixer! In other words I did not spend my evenings in the social club drinking and playing billiards, cards or darts. Had the job been offered to me, it is unlikely that I would have accepted, partly because I did not wish to spend the rest of my life in Australia and partly because, although the job was a good one and very well paid, I was in a position to know that my value to Lister's was, in fact, far greater than that of the Australasian representative could ever be, but really because I was a trained engineer acting as a salesman and general factotum and I was anxious to use my training. In the outcome, the appointment of Garlick's successor was to prove a turning point in my life, as you will read.

About the year 1930 Lister's were producing about 600 engines a week. Most of these were of small horsepower – 1½ hp to 3hp – and were largely used to power concrete mixers, stone crushers, air compressors and so on, and sales were handled by the Industrial Engineering Department. One of the largest users of these engines was Winget Ltd which made concrete mixers and allied lines at Warwick, which were sold by their London office in Grosvenor Square. The managing director was named Faulder Burn. He was a great friend of Percy Lister, who recognised him as a marvellous salesman but as a poor businessman who acted as a dictator and who had got his affairs into a muddle. At any given moment, they were heavily in debt to Lister, who stood to lose disastrously if anything went wrong with the conduct of the Winget business. It did.

Faulder Burn died suddenly – and intestate. Percy Lister realised he must do something immediately to prevent the possibility of a meeting of the creditors and the possible bankruptcy of the firm. Lister's were probably the largest creditor, and although this was not enough in itself to enable him to get control of the position, somehow he did: I can only conclude that he must have been given Power of Attorney by Mrs Faulder Burn, who I believe was the sole beneficiary. There was a close relationship between Percy Lister and Mrs Faulder Burn, who was paid a regular income as the result of some arrangement between them – until the Winget crisis was ended.

One day Percy Lister called me to his office and, after explaining the forego in confidence, although I already knew a lot of it, he said he wished me to go to London and take over the Winget office there. He gave me a sealed letter to present to Mr Cross, the director in charge. I never saw the letter but was informed that it instructed Mr Cross to surrender all books and records to me, and that he, his colleagues and staff were to carry out any instructions I might give. From the books and any information I could obtain I was to make a general assessment of the trading position, particularly the export side, which he felt it would be necessary for me to take over temporarily. I was to stay at any convenient hotel as long as it was necessary to do this.

I was astounded, as I had never had anything to do with the Winget business, and I had only been with Lister's for three years. However, I went the next day and booked in at the Rubens Hotel where I spent a comfortable three days.

Mr Cross, on receipt of the letter, proved to be very friendly and cooperative, so that I was able to get a general picture of the position very quickly. The financial

Lister's employees turning and grinding crankshafts (above), and (below) the Lister's sheep-shearing machine shop.

position was far too complicated for me to deal with, and I realised it would have to be sorted out at Dursley by the Accounts Department, but the export trade was most unsatisfactory and it was obvious that this would have to be put on a proper footing and be conducted from Dursley until a reasonable system had become routine. I therefore phoned Percy Lister, stated my opinion, and suggested that transport should be sent to collect all the books.

What happened to the home sales side of the business I do not know, or how the whole financial muddle was sorted out, but this was eventually done.

In the meantime the export trade was conducted from my office on the lines suggested by me, with a man named Webb in charge, and this was soon brought back to health. The report made by me to the directors is among my papers. I never received any financial reward for my efforts and I can't remember even having a thank you.

Looking back, it seems to me that whenever Lister's had some novel or unorthodox operation in mind, I got called in. The following is another case which had nothing to do with my department.

Some time after I joined Lister's they became part manufacturers and general distributors of a small three-wheel truck suitable for internal transport inside factories. The engine unit was built over the front driving wheel and the whole unit could be rotated, in a steel housing, through 360°. The patents were held by a firm at Norton St Philip, Somerset, called (I think) Auto Engineering Co. Ltd. They also made some of the specialized parts. These trucks gradually became quite popular, so much so that Lister's must have decided it would be advantageous for them to acquire the patents and take over all manufacturing.

Anyway, one day Percy Lister asked me to go with him to Bath and take with me any work I had scheduled for the day. So off we set in the Rolls-Royce and drew up in front of, I think, the Spa Hotel – the most exclusive hotel on the outskirts of Bath, where he was meeting the owners of the Auto-Truck. For the day I was to be his secretary and help him to impress the owners both of the hotel and the Auto-Truck. So as soon as the chauffeur-driven car stopped, Percy Lister charged up the steps into the hotel and I followed, clutching some files and papers. He got hold of the manager and asked him to provide me with an office and a typewriter. The manager said the only office he had was the one he was using, so Percy Lister said 'All right, we shall have to do with that, so will you remove anything you will be wanting but leave a good typewriter.' Within minutes I was installed and at work.

Percy Lister rushed off to his meeting, but before he went he said he would be sending a messenger in due course for me to bring in all the letters and documents I wanted him to sign, and he wanted the quantity to be impressive, even if it meant including a few items that didn't really need his signature.

So two or three hours passed with me wondering what Percy Lister was up to, and trying to give an impression of concentrated busy-ness. It was early evening before I got the message and proceeded to the room where the meeting had been held, with a pile of letters and documents which Percy Lister signed at great speed. He then introduced me to the directors of Auto Engineering, after which I took the draft agreement as modified in discussion and made a final copy for signature. I took this back to the room where it was stamped and signed, and I was given a substantial draught of whisky.

That agreement transferred all the patents, drawings and rights in the Auto-Truck to Lister's, and they had it at a bargain price. I immediately saw that all present were drunk except Percy Lister, and he was nearly so. You can draw your own conclusions as to his tactics. I should have been very drunk too if I had had half the liquor I was offered.

Fortunately the chauffeur was sober so we got home safely. On the way home Percy Lister was very amused at the show we had put up and pleased with the bargain he had pulled off, but finally spent the latter part of the journey asleep with his head on my shoulder.

On several occasions I accompanied Percy Lister to London, and worked on the train. We would catch the Cheltenham Flyer (then the fastest train in the world) leaving Stroud at 3.16 p.m. and arriving in Paddington at 5.00 p.m. and having tea on the way. I would normally return on the 6.35 p.m. but on one occasion I broke the world record for a stay in London. It lasted minus two minutes, for we actually arrived four minutes earlier than the official time of 5.00 p.m., and I ran round and caught the Cheltenham Express which left dead on the scheduled time of 5.00 p.m.!

We did several working car journeys too – when he used his smaller 20hp Rolls, as all his other assistants got car sickness in that particular car.

About two years after I had taken over Australasian sales, a large percentage of which was accounted for by sheep-shearing machinery, I had occasion to look at the accounts and found that agents had been underpaying for a considerable period. The pricing was a bit complicated, so that the error was not easy to detect, and when I reported it to Percy Lister I had a job to convince him that I was right. At first he decided to let it go, but when I said it amounted to a total of £4,000, he decided to write to them as politely as possible (as they were agents whose business we could not afford to lose) and point out what had happened. They all wrote back (including our representative Mr Garlick, who had not then met me), rejecting the case we had put forward and damning me by bell, book and candle for suggesting such a thing.

Percy Lister showed me the letters and said, 'Who am I to believe, you or them? You have only been on this job for a couple of years, and they have been doing it for many years. Not only so, but they all agree, including Garlick.'

I said, 'That is so, but it doesn't alter the fact that I am right, as you will find if you get our accountant to carefully check the accounts covering these transactions.'

This inspection proved to Percy Lister that I was right beyond all doubt and the agents had to pay up. By this piece of detection on my part I secured to Lister's money well in excess of all the wages they had paid me during all the years I worked for them – but I got nothing. However, this was one of several occasions where Percy Lister backed me in an argument even against his brothers. It is a remarkable fact, and one that I much appreciated.

As I write this record I am beginning to wonder how I did any of the ordinary work for which I was paid, for in addition to the special jobs I have referred to I was frequently called upon to act as a guide to parties going round the works.

Overseas representatives usually spent a week or two in my office to learn how we conducted our export business. Three of these were very interesting. Some time before I joined the firm a man named Callard went to R.A. Lister House, Canada, with a letter which he presented to the then managing director, dismissing that gentleman and appointing himself (Callard) in his place. Some years later I was introduced to Lt Col Wilmot, who had been the youngest Canadian battalion commander in the Great War and afterwards became head of the Canadian Customs in Britain. Percy Lister said he was to stay with me for two to three weeks, and was then to take Callard's place in Canada. Sure enough, he took Callard a letter similar to the one Callard had himself taken, who was dismissed and replaced by Wilmot. About three years later Wilmot was himself replaced and set up a small private business in Toronto as a customs advisor.

Another case of a most extraordinary character was that of L.A. Poole. Percy Lister rang for me one day and when I arrived in his office he asked if I knew a man named Poole who was assisting Sanders (our engine designer). I said I did not. He continued, 'Well never mind, but the fact is that he has fallen foul of one of my brothers and is under notice to leave. He has a month to go, which he has to work out, but we can't let him stay with Sanders and get a lot of technical information which he can sell elsewhere. So he had better spend the month in your office.'

I said, 'Well, what am I supposed to do with him?', to which Percy Lister replied that he was an expert technical illustrator and as I was responsible for the instruction books I could use him for any illustrations I thought necessary. I asked when he was to start and was told 'Now. Go to the drawing office and fetch him.'

I felt very puzzled and unhappy but I had no option but to do as I was told. So I went to Sanders' office and asked for Mr Poole, to whom I was introduced. I told Sanders of my instructions, and asked Poole to collect up all his belongings and come with me. He was stunned, but did as I asked him and on the way I told him I didn't know why the move was taking place, and I didn't want to know. All that I asked was that he should quietly work out his notice helping me with the engine instruction books. He said he would, but insisted on explaining that Robert Lister had offered him the lease of a house that he (Robert) owned at the bottom of Long Street, Dursley, but it was so badly situated and in such a condition that he (Poole) had refused it. This had apparently led to a blazing row, in which Poole had told Robert where he got off and Robert had insisted on his dismissal.

I tried to console him, and we got along fine. I quickly learnt that he was nationally known in the automotive industry. He was the designer of the first Karrier 'camel' and had had numerous technical illustrations published in the motoring journals. I hadn't enough work to keep him fully occupied, but he did some very useful illustrations.

One day he said he was not feeling well and asked if he could go the work's clinic and get attention. I said, 'Of course', and off he went. My office was on the second floor and the door from the corridor had glass in the upper panels. Shortly after Poole had gone, George Lister, who had nothing to do with my department, came charging in and shouted, 'Haven't you got a man named Poole in this office?' I said 'Yes', and he shouted, 'Where is he?', to which I could only reply that he had gone to the clinic as he was unwell. George retorted, 'He isn't in the clinic. He's standing in the yard watching an Auto-Truck being tried out. He is to come back immediately and not to leave in working hours without your express permission.'

George departed and Poole returned. I said, 'Where have you been?', and he said, 'To the clinic, of course, as I asked you.' 'Haven't you been watching an Auto-Truck being tried out in the yard?' I asked. Poole replied, 'Yes, I did look at one for a minute. I hadn't seen one before; but what of it, and how do you know?' I then told him of George's visit, at which he looked at me and said, 'So I'm your prisoner. I never dreamt I'd come to this.' And he went to his desk and sat down and sobbed. I felt dreadful, to see a man of his standing, about fifty-five years of age, in that condition. So I explained the Lister psychology and said, 'I don't trouble when you go out or what you do, so long as you keep clear of the directors, and while you are in the office you appear to be hard at work, because there is clear glass on that door, which they will not fail to look through every time they pass.'

I understand that Poole went back to the motor trade, and there is a letter from him among my papers with an article illustrated by him.

The third man was a Major Parsons, brother of the Mayor of Worcester and a tank expert in the First World War. He was European general manager of Millars Machinery Co., with headquarters in Paris, when Percy Lister met him and encouraged him to join Lister's on the promise that he would be given charge of all our operations in West Africa.

He took up residence in my office for two or three months, during which he visited and spent some time in each department learning all about our products, and finally being instructed by me in our business methods, particularly in respect of exports. Apparently he had been given a definite period for training, the end of which passed without any arrangements being made for his departure to West Africa.

I was very puzzled about all this, as practically all our West African trade was handled by a subsidiary of Lever Brothers and there was no need for a representative. So when he became worried as to what was happening I said, 'You can forget all about West Africa for I am sure Lister's haven't the slightest idea of sending you there, and they never had. Now they don't know what to do with you.' He stayed for weeks, doing nothing on a salary several times bigger than mine, and at last we decided to break with Lister's and set up a business partnership, of which more anon.

I must mention one other man of some standing whose life was ruined by Lister's. His name was Campbell and he was the son of the founder of the once-famous Campbell Engine Co.

One day, entering Percy Lister's office, I saw him sitting in the sunshine on the blue settee under the window. He was very fair, tall and handsome, and he looked as though he was about to enter the Promised Land. I thought, 'I wonder what doom awaits him at the hands of Lister's.' I had my answer a few years later, when having acted as our representative in the West Indies, and having been sacked, he shot himself in a London street.

Although I could write a lot more about my time at Lister's it would be more a story of the firm than of my connection with it. So I will content myself with briefly recording that I acted as a guide to the works for visiting parties; wrote articles in trade magazines; presented the case for a tariff on foreign separators for the Ottowa Conference; met the Australian Customs Minister in London and got a number of our products exempted from the Australian customs tariff; was involved in the introduction of the stainless steel bowl in cream separators; was the Dursley liaison in respect of exports during the negotiations with Ruston Hornsby with a view to merger; took charge of all the Asian and Australasian business during Percy Lister's trip round the world; later took over sales to Canada and Africa; and, finally, was also secretary of the tennis club.

While working at Lister's I suggested to the Australian Literature Society that they hold an Australian Book Week at Australia House in London, which I helped to organise. The committee met at Australia House under the chairmanship of the High Commissioner, Sir Granville Ryrie. The event was so successful that it was extended to a fortnight. Lister's did not have the slightest idea that I was involved in this. The secretary of the society sent me a book entitled *An Australian Garden of Prose* as a memento.

It was during my period at Lister's that the great international financial crisis took place, with the collapse of the New York Stock Market. All the foreign exchanges went crazy, and the Australian banks were unable to obtain English currency for their customers to pay our account. As a result we arranged for our Australian agents to pay us in wool, which we sold in Bradford at a considerable loss.

From about 1935 Percy Lister spent less and less time at Dursley and more on dealings outside the firm. This worried me because I knew that without his protection my job was very insecure. George, Robert and Frank Lister were all afraid and jealous of Percy. They regarded me as his chief executive for schemes and stunts of his, of which they did not approve, so much so that one day he said to me, 'My brothers don't seem to like you. They say you are difficult to get on with. What do you say to that?' I replied that I was not surprised 'in view of the number of times I have had to cross swords with them to carry out your instructions, but if my performance is satisfactory to you it doesn't really matter.' 'OK', he said, 'But don't fall out with them too much.'

Major Parsons and I had already foreseen the possibility of my getting the sack, and had an understanding that we would set up an agency business on our own.

The position as representative for Australia and New Zealand was still vacant. I knew from Garlick that I had been considered for this but had been turned down for reasons already stated. So I was not surprised that one day, during one of Percy Lister's long absences, a man turned up who I understood was to be groomed for the Australian vacancy. He started to deal with all the Australian correspondence and to give me instructions as to how Australian matters should be dealt with. I received no information from the directors as to what was happening, but after a few days, on being told to do something by this man (whose name I never knew), I said, 'Look, Mister, I don't know who you are or what authority you have, but so far as I am concerned you are telling your grandmother how to suck eggs. I am not prepared to receive any orders from you and you can go to Hell.'

He departed. I was called to the board room where there were George, Robert and Frank. George asked me whether this was really what I had said. I told him, 'Yes', and was instantly dismissed with one week's pay.

Thus ended ten and a half years of extreme variety and interest, with an extraordinary firm which on the whole was very efficient. But, alas, it was also a firm in which no one ever felt safe.

The board room at the Priory in the late 1920s. It looks almost identical eighty years later.

Eleven

Engineering a Living

Our England is a garden, and such gardens are not made
By singing – 'Oh, how beautiful!' and sitting in the shade,
While better men than we go out and start their working lives
At grubbing weeds from gravel paths with broken dinner knives.

(Rudyard Kipling)

Although Vera could not have been very surprised at my parting with Lister's, she was very upset when it actually came and at the manner in which it took place. She could never really reconcile herself to the fact that without Percy Lister there was no future for me at Lister's.

As previously agreed, Parsons and I went into partnership as a sales agency bringing in specialised lines from abroad, particularly the Kinkade single-wheeled garden tractor, which was made in Minneapolis. We also took over the sales of concrete moulds made by Whitfields, iron founders and engineers of Dudbridge, Stroud, and we rented an office on their premises.

In August 1936 we registered a private limited company under the name of Bullock, Parsons and Company Limited, with an authorised capital of £1,000 in £1 shares. Parsons took 400 of these and I had 400, purchased with a loan of £400 from Vera's parents, pending the sale of Yartleton. I commuted to Stroud each day and Parsons lived in digs, going to Worcester (where his brother was mayor) every weekend.

Vera and I started to look for a suitable house in Stroud, and at the suggestion of Vera's parents we tried to get one which could be divided into two, as these larger houses could be obtained at a much cheaper figure (relatively) than the much more popular three-bedroom size. We found the ideal house at 63, Stratford Road, Stroud, and with the proceeds of Yartleton (which we sold to a friend – Mr Ball of Cam – for around £700) and the proceeds of Lynwood (about £800), plus a mortgage, we were able to cover all the financial arrangements.

Mr Wyatt was greatly looking forward to the move to Stroud and visited the house two or three times on a bicycle. The move was arranged to take place during the August Bank Holiday week of 1937, but, alas, on the Bank Holiday Sunday I had to take Mr Wyatt into Bristol Royal Infirmary for an emergency operation from which he never recovered. He died in hospital a few weeks later without ever taking up residence in Stroud.

Brimscombe (in 1906), where Arthur set up Bullock, Parsons & Co. in the mid-1930s. It is a happy coincidence that his factory at Port Mill is now occupied by The History Press at the time when they are publishing his book!

Under the circumstances there was no point in dividing the accommodation, so Mrs Wyatt lived with us. Every Sunday, and sometimes during the week, she attended Castle Street Methodist Chapel – a walk of a mile and a half up a very steep hill.

When we moved to Stroud Nancy was seven, and went to Uplands Primary School. Fortunately she had several companions and this was lucky as it was about a mile up and down each way, with several dangerous road crossings and corners. I mention it because she became great friends with a girl called Pamela Iles, who was the niece of Laurie Lee, the author of *Cider With Rosie*. Laurie Lee had also been a pupil at Uplands. Nancy stayed at Uplands until she was eleven and then won a scholarship to Stroud Girls' High School but did not qualify for a free place because our income was too high.

For the first year the business in Stroud just about held its own, but it was a bit of a struggle. About the end of 1937 Major Parsons received a letter from the War Office requesting him to report. I never did know exactly what the contents of that letter were, but I think he must have been on some special reserve. At that time the government was preparing itself for war with Hitler's Germany, and I knew that Parsons was a tank expert. He had to go, and I never heard from him again.

The building owned by Whitfield in which we had rented an office had originally been the foundry of the ill-fated Hampton Car Company of Dudbridge. It was my intention to build up a business in the sale and (if possible) the manufacture of a range of horticultural machines, but we had to start operating before I had been able to negotiate agencies, so our only lines for the first year were pumps and the concrete moulds made by Whitfilelds, which was much too small a basis. However, I was negotiating for the sales agency for the British Isles of the Kinkade garden tractor, and this I eventually secured. In the meantime I had been asked by a firm occupying part of Port Mills, Brimscombe (a disused stone-built cloth mill), if I could help them with the sales of the automatic coin-operated slot machines they were making.

This came about through a friendship I had struck up with Mr W. Waddington – an electrician who was doing some work for Whitfields. He explained that part of his time was spent on the electrical work necessary for the automatic machines, but although these machines were very good apparently, the more the company sold, the bigger became their financial difficulties, so that they could not invest in more plant or more labour, and were about to stop manufacture. He asked if I would go to Brimscombe and discuss with the proprietors, Mrs Reed and her son, how to get out of this extraordinary position and put the business on a working basis. This I did, and found the Reeds a very charming and well-educated pair. They provided me with all the facts. It became quickly apparent that they were attempting the arithmetically impossible. The machines were sold through a hire purchase company under an arrangement which meant that, for this facility, the finance company retained an amount larger than the net profit which could be achieved on the sale, and the amount they actually paid was so delayed that Reeds were starved of money for materials and wages.

I went to London and obtained a much more favourable and workable arrangement, but it was too late. The creditors would not wait to give the new arrangement a chance and the automatic machine company went into liquidation. However, Waddington suggested that as the premises were very much larger and better than those I occupied at Dudbridge, and there was a small amount of plant going for a song, that I should take over. He would join Bullock, Parsons & Co. Ltd, who would take on electrical contracting and engineering jobbing; and we would invite Mr C.T.R. Shepheard, who was connected with the Reeds but who was operating a small sign manufacturing company separately in the same building, to join us. Shepheard was the son of a bank manager in Poole, Dorset, and a trained engineer. Waddington had considerable mechanical engineering experience as well as electrical, so I thought the link up could be mutually advantageous. They both became directors of Bullock, Parsons & Co. Ltd and we took over substantial factory space and offices at Port Mills, Brimscombe. We seriously got down to running a somewhat mixed manufacturing concern, with me as chairman and managing director.

While all this was going on I had secured the sales rights for the British Isles of the Kinkade garden tractor to which I have already referred, and was achieving a steady sale. The one difficulty I was up against was that the Kinkade people insisted on cash with order. This meant that we had to obtain our own order before ordering from America, which meant delivery in four to eight weeks, or alternatively the risk of ordering a stock from America which meant the locking up of most of our small capital. However, this was what we were forced to do until the increase in business involved us in paying in advance a sum which was unreasonable, and we finally persuaded the Kinkade people to maintain a stock in bond in Southampton on which we could draw, paying cash as we did so.

We continued making and selling a few signs and did some other engineering odd jobs – several for a Mr Mortimer, who had a prosperous wood turnery business

The Kinkade garden tractor which Arthur was licensed to sell in the British Isles.

just along the canal. One day he showed me a German machine for dipping handles in paint a gross at a time. The withdrawal was by a balance weight, but the speed of withdrawal was so slow that the handles were almost completely dry on full withdrawal and beautifully finished. He said he wanted another machine but could not get one from Germany (just before the war) and could I make one?

I gave this some thought and consulted Waddington and Shepheard with the suggestion of controlling the fall of the weight by use of a hydraulic cylinder with a very finely controlled outflow. They thought it would work and I took the chance of designing and making six. This strained our small production resources. We already had one employee and we put on one or two more, but it was becoming obvious that we must have a draughtsman, though there was not quite enough work available to justify his wages. I can't remember how, but I was introduced to a young man from Bristol named Holloway who was training as a designer of organs. He could not see any future in that and wanted a change. He wasn't qualified in engineering and I could not afford to pay him much for his limited skill. However, in order to get the opportunity of learning without being too exacting, he agreed to come to Brimscombe for a very low wage for a limited period. It turned out to be one of the best investments that either he or I could have made.

Everybody knew that war was in the offing. The government was preparing, and, apart from placing orders for war materials and armaments, was issuing orders which greatly affected business. When war was declared on 3 September 1939 we had a small staff doing the work I have already described. I remember sitting in the front window of my office at Port Mills on that Sunday and hearing the declaration of war read by Neville Chamberlain on a radio set I had taken over for that purpose. I was quite alone, and I realised that it meant great changes – one of which was that we could no longer import Kinkade tractors and would have to make them.

Until we were forced to do something else we could only continue what we were doing, but I got into touch with the Kinkade people in America, explained the position and asked for manufacturing rights, which they granted, and helped us to get into production by supplying drawings and special spare parts. Manufacture involved the making of a special integral engine and was a major undertaking for a well-equipped firm, but within a year we had patterns made and produced our first machines using some American spare parts.

It may strain the credulity of the reader to know that the first machine was produced by us on plant costing less than £10, namely: a 4in Duncan lathe belonging to Waddington, an old horizontal mill we bought for £4 and a 3/4in pillar drill, belt driven, which had been left in the mill when it was abandoned. This first Kinkade was sold to a nurseryman named Cox at the Quarry, Stinchcombe, and proved to be the foundation of his business.

While this was going on I had ordered forward some machines to be put into Southampton in bond for me to draw on, and in so doing I confess I was knowingly contravening the law, for the government, in order to conserve exchange, had issued an order forbidding such imports except under licence. However, I could not afford to have our main source of income stopped. I knew there would be trouble, but thought I could bluff it out.

The tractors duly arrived and I applied for their release. This was refused and I was referred to the Department of Trade. I decided to elicit the help of the Department of Agriculture, but they were not very friendly and implied that it served me right. So I requested an interview at the Ministry of Agriculture.

At various tractor demonstrations I had become friendly with a Mr M. Meyer, a Swiss who had introduced the Simas Rotary Horticultural Tractor to Britain and who was generally acknowledged to be the greatest living authority on garden tractors. I wrote asking him to meet me outside the Ministry of Agriculture at the appointed time, which he did. I told him very briefly what the position was, but asked him not to say anything except when I asked him to do so. He agreed, and we met a senior official of the Ministry who lost no time in giving me a good dressing down for breach of the law. I could only plead inadvertence and apologise, but pointed out that the machines were in Southampton, and food growers in Britain were anxious to get hold of them to produce something to keep us all alive. I also mentioned that I had brought with me the leading expert on small tractors who would explain to the Ministry why these tractors were special and why they should be released as quickly as possible. I said the position was unfortunate, but the problem must be resolved. However, our interviewer again refused, and said the law had been broken and it was more than his job was worth to condone it.

I said we seemed to have gone as far as we could, and thanked the official for his patience and sympathy, adding that there was nothing left for me to do but to call public attention to this ridiculous situation. He looked a bit startled and asked what I meant by that, to which I replied that I intended when I left the office to go straight to the *Daily Mail* and tell them the whole story of how red tape was being used to prevent machines being put into action for the production of badly wanted food.

That was enough. He sprang into action. 'There is no need to do that', he said, 'Everybody has got the wrong ideas about civil servants. We can be as reasonable and as quick off the mark as anyone else when the need arises.' And to prove it he sent a clerk to fetch some papers and files which he pored over for a few minutes. He then said he was anxious to help and thought he saw a way out. I never did know what the way out was, but the outcome was that we left with an authorisation for the machines to be released immediately. He also remembered some relations he had in the Cotswolds and spoke of his love for that part of the country.

Some years later, when we resumed sales of Kinkades after the war, Meyer joined our staff as a salesman and demonstrator.

Twelve

Many Parts

Life is a privilege. Like some rare rose
The mysteries of the human mind unclose
What marvels lie in earth, and air, and sea!
What stores of knowledge wait our opening key!
What sunny roads of happiness lead out
Beyond the realms of indolence and doubt!
And what large pleasures smile upon and bless
The busy avenues of usefulness!

(Ella Wheeler Wilcox)

The advent of war was to mean great change in many directions. We were asked by the Government to form and train a small group of employees for the defence of the works against any landing of German paratroopers. This group numbered eight, and the foreman, Mills, was put in charge. Our arms consisted of a German Manser rifle from the First World War and a double-barrelled .410 ratting pistol. We had regular meetings to decide on duties, defensive dispositions and possible hand weapons. Firing practice took place in a long building with steel doors at one end which made an ideal shooting gallery. Unfortunately, while Mills was alright with the rifle, he could not be persuaded to handle the ratting pistol. These works groups were called the L.D.V. and were later organised into the Home Guard.

I volunteered as a part-time, unpaid fireman, and in this capacity much of my spare time was taken up with drills, lectures and later with air-raid alerts and actual fires. I was largely responsible for the establishment and training of fire-fighting teams in many Cotswold villages, equipped with simple hand appliances. This took me all over the central Cotswolds, which I travelled at my own expense, the only help I got being an extra supply of petrol coupons.

Among the many interesting people I met while involved in this task were those at the Whiteway Colony near Miserden. This was a colony of communist idealists from London, consisting of (I believe) seven men and two women. One of these was Nellie Shaw, with whom I became very friendly, and who wrote the fascinating story of their struggle for existence, a version of which appeared on television in 1982.

My experiences as a fireman would take too long to relate, but what I chiefly remember is the driving: I drove every sort of vehicle, with gears going in all directions,

Service was an important part of Arthur and Vera's lives in both war and peacetime. The bottom two items in the upper photo are Arthur's Gloucestershire Regiment and Ox. and Bucks cap badges from the First World War. The image also shows Arthur's Civil Defence Corps badge (top left) and a badge recalling Vera's many years working for the Womens Institute (top right). The bottom two photos show Arthur's badges from the National Fire Service and Auxiliary Fire Service, as well as Vera's Women's Voluntary Service badge.

and in all states of mechanical fitness, sometimes with only side lights and sometimes with lights which went on and off. Even at best one could hardly see to drive because, in accordance with the blackout restrictions, the headlights of all cars had to be covered by metal masks which projected a minimum of light on to the road through slits in the front. Most of the mobile pumps were drawn by large motor cars, and we drivers became very wary of some of them. One – a Ford V8 – was particularly notorious. It had no starter or starting handle. The steering was faulty and it only had side lights. Once it had been started by pushing, it had to be left running and became nearly red hot. The first time I had to drive it was in the middle of an air raid over Stroud, when I was ordered to take a team in the vehicle to a small fire in the district. It had been left running in the street outside the station, and I can remember walking up the path and looking up to see a German bomber caught in the apex of the searchlights directly overhead. I hardly need say the journey was a nightmare.

Travelling at night was very difficult, what with the blacked out headlights, no sign posts and people deliberately misdirecting you in case you were Germans. Once, coming back from a journey to Leicester, we missed Stroud and ended up

Arthur and Vera's
daughter Nancy in 1941,
aged eleven.

near Swindon. Wherever I went on these expeditions I carried the aforementioned double-barrelled ratting pistol, loaded, in the pocket of the car door.

Before the start of the war the Stroud district had been designated as a reception area for evacuees from Birmingham. Soon after the war commenced a whole girls' grammar school and all the parents connected with it came down and were billeted in private homes. At 63, Stratford Road, we had six bedrooms and a basement. Two attic rooms were occupied by a lady named Miss Leakey as a miniature flat, but we had to find accommodation for two of the schoolgirls, aged about sixteen, and their mother, who proved to be the wife of a German Jew who had fled from Germany and set up a pencil factory in Birmingham.

It was somewhat crowded and a bit hectic, but we all got on very well together. The school alternated with Stroud Girls' High School for lessons. Vera was a helper on the services canteen in Stroud and helped with the school dinners. Everybody did war work of some sort.

A lot of evacuees also came from London and many were allotted to the outlying villages. They came to Stroud station carrying their most treasured possessions in all sorts of bags and boxes – grandmothers, babies and all. They gathered temporarily in schools and church halls, whence they were taken to the villages by volunteer car owners, including me.

They all looked very pathetic and I felt so sorry for them, but there was some amusement too. One journey I made was with a mixed party of eight from the East End of London to the home of Sir W. Rosenthal, the well-known portrait painter, at Oakridge. My car was overloaded with people, and with their belongings draped all over the car, including a parrot in a cage, I was doubtful about ever getting to Oakridge. We did, but when we reached the open spaces on the top of the Cotswolds there were lamentations from the children about the absence of shops. The Rosenthal home was a real Cotswold establishment furnished with antiques and red Turkey rugs on bare stone floors. I have often wondered what the evacuees made of it and how they all got on together.

The people from Birmingham did not stay very long, but after them we had a procession of tenants in the basement, including an officer's wife and daughter named Baines, and Ilsa Leven, who was a German refugee working as a secretary for Ruberoid.

At the factory at Brimscombe we carried on with the manufacture of Kinkades and other lines, gradually building up our plant and staff, but it was getting harder to obtain materials, especially the special alloy steels required for gears and so on, so we asked the Kinkade people in America if they could let us have some of these special parts. It must have been after Dunkirk and the commencement of the bombing of London and other cities because the reply that came back must surely have been one of the most sentimental business letters ever written. I can't remember the exact words, but the following is a fairly accurate paraphrase:

> Yes, we will let you have the parts you ask for, even if we have to go out and strip them off machines in use, after the magnificent fight you are putting up. Our hearts go out to you as every day we listen anxiously to the radio and read the papers to see if you are still holding out.

I replied to thank him both for the parts and for the sentiments he expressed. I said I was publishing his letter in the local paper and in return I wanted him to publish mine in the Minneapolis paper. I told him he was unduly anxious, that everybody here was in good spirits and that there was no question of defeat, because no matter who was against us or for us we would continue until we won: the British always win one battle in a war – the last one, and that is the only one which counts.

However, it was not long after this that the war really caught up with us.

My secretary came in from answering the door one day to say that three men wished to see me urgently. I went out to find three men in bowler hats standing on the doorstep. They identified themselves as top officials of the Ministry of Aircraft Production and showed me their authority to commandeer any personnel or property they wished. They explained that there were hundreds of aeroplanes completed but unable to fly due to the lack of instruments such as automatic pilots, which were being made by the Sperry Gyroscope Company at Stonehouse (about four miles away). It was vital that their output should be immediately increased many times over, and they were combing all the local engineering works for the necessary machinists not engaged on work of equal priority. They requested me to accompany them round the works and explain the task that each machinist was engaged on and its relative importance. They would decide what was to happen to each employee.

This I did, and they took about six of our best machinists, to each of whom they said, 'You are being transferred to Sperry Gyroscope. Collect up your tools, get your hat and coat and wait outside for a car which will collect you in a few minutes. You will not come back here, and no objections will be accepted.'

I was stunned. I sent for Shepheard and Waddington, and when I had explained what had happened they were equally shocked. It was obvious that if we were to remain in business we had to drop the work we were doing and get some of top priority, though we should have to take a chance on our ability to do the work with our best men gone.

Although I had been warned about the dangers of subcontracting to the Bristol Aeroplane Co., I had no option and immediately got in touch with them over the phone. They told us to come on down and select the sort of work we could undertake.

So the next day Waddington and I went down to Bristol and looked through the pile of work they had on offer. We came back with enough orders to keep us going for a long time, enough of the top priority to necessitate searching for more skilled workers. We were told that one of these orders was especially urgent and they asked to get them machined and down to Bristol with the utmost speed. The order was for seventy-seven connectors about 1½in long. These parts were immediately machined, and (remembering the reputation of B.A.C. for ruthless inspection) we inspected them carefully to ensure that they were correct. Having satisfied ourselves on this we sent them by carrier to Bristol, but did not proceed with any more work until we knew that they had been accepted. In other words, we decided to treat this as a test case. Two or three days later we received them back with a reject note which applied to the whole batch.

I immediately got on the phone to the man who had placed the orders making the special request for speed, told him they had all been rejected, and said that I had cancelled all the thousands of pounds worth of orders they had placed with us and was returning the drawings.

He said, 'You can't do that.' I replied, 'Can't I? I've done it.'

A couple of hours later we had a phone call from Brown, the works director, asking us to delay cancelling the orders, and requesting us to bring the parts down to Bristol for inspection and discussion. So Waddington and I went down and met with a panel of experts, with Brown in the chair and including the chief inspector, whose name was Bush. He was notorious among my engineering friends. The parts were checked for dimensions with micrometers and proved to be correct, so Brown asked why they had been rejected. Bush did not know and would have to find the person who did the actual inspection. As this might take some time Brown suggested an adjournment for a cup of tea, but before we adjourned I asked where on the aeroplane the connectors were used. Nobody knew. This annoyed Brown, who said that during the adjournment this information must be obtained.

When we reassembled, the actual inspector was asked to explain the inspection. He pointed to the alternate light and dark patches made by the milling cutter in cutting a concave piece out of the end of the connectors. I said this was absolute rubbish as the marks were what is known as 'witness marks', which are always present when a milling cutter of that type is used, and it is impossible to carry out the operation without leaving them. They were not of the slightest importance for two reasons: firstly, because they were immeasurable, and secondly, because even had this not been true, it would not matter two hoots as the concave mouth was to be fitted over a fuel pipe to which it was to be brazed. A draughtsman confirmed that this was so. At this, Brown lost his temper and gave the inspectors a good dressing down for causing all this delay. He apologised to us, asked us to proceed with the other orders we had, and also asked if he could come up to our works the following Sunday.

We had lunch at the Imperial and continued our conversation at the works, where Brown confessed to me that he had been worried for some time at the enormous amount of work that was being rejected by their inspectors. Not only was it causing a lot of trouble with sub-contractors and wasting valuable materials, but is was gravely interfering with production and the flow of work. Our complaint and visit to Bristol had revealed the trouble and given him a lever to get things altered. He said that most of their inspectors were recruited from butchers, bakers and candlestick makers who knew nothing about engineering, but had gone through a short course of training which made them proficient in reading micrometers and other measuring instruments but nothing else. He had provisionally decided (following our visit) to set up a salvage department manned by experienced engineers, to whom all rejected work would be submitted, and who would judge if the grounds for rejection made the parts unfit for use. He wanted my opinion and criticism of the plan. I said I thought it an excellent idea. He rang me up some time later to say the scheme was working like a charm and that they had salvaged about two-thirds of the rejects amounting to hundreds of thousands of pounds' worth of work.

After that we got on excellently with B.A.C., and were informed that although we were not by any means their biggest subcontractors, we stood in first place for accuracy, speed of delivery and minimum waste of materials.

We also machined a lot of aeroplane engine parts for Rolls-Royce, with whom we had the same reputation! In fact, we were the sole producers of certain parts for the two most famous engines of the war: six for the Bristol Hercules rotary and five for the Rolls-Royce Merlin in-line, the latter being the Spitfire engine.

In addition to this, we machined gun mountings for Humber and our sheet metal and welding department made hundreds of units for producing gas as an alternative to petrol for driving motor cars. We had ten women gas welders engaged on nothing else.

In connection with the appointment of one of these women there is rather an amusing story. Brimscombe is one of a string of villages on the London Road from Stroud, and to get to our factory from this road one had to take a side road over a humpbacked canal bridge, the factory gate being close to the bridge. We had put an advert for welders in the local paper, and I was standing in the office behind my seated secretary, looking out of the window at this bridge. A woman appeared carrying a shopping bag and turned in at the gate.

I casually said, 'Here's the first would-be welder in answer to our advert. She doesn't live in Brimscombe but in Thrupp or Chalford, most likely Chalford. She has been into Stroud shopping and she decided to drop off and enquire about a job. She doesn't know what door to apply to, and will go round the end of the machine shop.'

The woman duly disappeared around the corner.

I said, 'By now she has found her error and before I count four she will appear again round the end of the shop and come down to the arch then walk up to the front door, so you can go to the door and let her in.'

This my secretary did, but she looked white-faced and frightened when she returned. She said, 'You must be clairvoyant or you know the woman for it is exactly as you said.' I could only reply that I wasn't and I didn't, pointing out how easily simple deduction could be mistaken for clairvoyance.

The gun mounting that we machined for Humber was half a steel ball about 6in in diameter, and on top of this was another solid piece of steel in which we had to carve a circular concave hollow to fit on the ball exactly, to form a swivel. This job was beyond the capacity of any of our machines and it was almost beyond our technical capacity too. However, we thought we could do it if we could get a big enough machine so Waddington, and I went to Birmingham and bought a big second-hand lathe for £500 (which was many thousands of pounds in today's money). The purchase price was as much as we could afford, and we were taking quite a chance. Unfortunately, while on the way to Brimscombe the lorry carrying the lathe skidded on the icy road and crashed, throwing the lathe off and severely damaging it. The carriers had not insured it and we had not dreamt of doing so. It cost us a considerable amount to get it collected and delivered and so, what with that and the cost of repairs, we were faced with a very substantial loss. However, we eventually got it going and the special attachment for cutting the concave hollow worked perfectly. It is interesting to record that Humbers were well aware of how formidable was the task of machining this mounting, and to assist us they arranged with the Gloster Aircraft Company – who had taken over the carpet factory of Bond Worth as the secret tool room for tooling up the first jet plane, the Meteor – to permit us to inspect the machining of a similar job which was being done there. Shepheard, Waddington and I visited the factory by appointment and carefully inspected the job. We found that it was almost identical to the one we had to do, but about half the size and set up in a special fixture on a huge horizontal ward lathe, which cost at least ten times as much as the lathe we were going to use. We learnt that the special fixture for holding the job had cost more than our lathe and fixture put together. We wrote a letter of thanks to Humber, and carried on in our own way.

Although it seems crazy to say so, and a contradiction in terms, the second half of the war, when the military situation had turned in favour of the Allies, was a period of peace. Life had dropped into a steady routine, and in spite of shortages and restrictions people were happy, and also close together because of having to create their own amusements and share common burdens. For our firm it was a period of prosperity, having a continuous run of profitable work. This continued right up to the end of the war, when readjustments had to be made.

Before I conclude my remarks on war work I must allude to an opportunity we had to make a tidy but legitimate profit, to offset some of the lines which were not so lucrative. The big firms like B.A.C., Rolls-Royce and Humber had liaison men going round to their subcontractors to keep things moving and to smooth out any snags. They were supposed to be able to advise on selecting a machine and the best way of using it. The only man who could do this successfully was the one from Rolls-Royce. When he called he went straight to the machines being employed on Rolls-Royce jobs and criticised and advised. Then, without stopping for a conversation or a cup of tea, he went back to his car and drove off. By contrast, the B.A.C. man, who was very friendly, spent most of his time in the office and always had a cup of tea.

Shortly before the end of the war, B.A.C. developed an engine called the Taurus, which was to make all other engines out of date. Calling on us one day, the B.A.C. man produced some rough stamping and a drawing of a small lever which was an essential part of the Taurus, of which a quantity were urgently required. He asked if we would machine them and at what price. I called in Waddington and we examined the stampings and drawing and found that out of a rough stamping we had to produce a machined part of extreme accuracy. The difficulty was that the stamping did not seem to have enough metal to give a reasonable margin for machining and being rough gave no field point or surface for location. However, after some consideration Waddington and I agreed on a method of tackling the problem and machining a quantity of, say, twenty-four at a time. I asked the B.A.C. man why he had come to us, as we were not the biggest of the B.A.C. subcontractors or the most favoured.

I added, 'You have already approached some of the others haven't you, as we see from the sample that somebody has tried to do the job and failed?'

He confessed that this was so and said he had been instructed to approach us as we had never failed yet. So I told him we would do the job provided the order was for a minimum of 2,000, but that we were not going to quote a price until we knew how the levers had been machined and how much it had cost, based on the sample engines already in use. He said those levers had to be handmade in the B.A.C. tool room because nobody else could machine them, but they couldn't afford the waste of time in the tool room any longer.

We told him to phone Bristol and find out what the machining had cost. He said each one had taken half an hour and the labour cost was 2/6½ but he wanted it done for less. I replied that as it was impossible for him to get them machined for less, that would be the price; and so it was. The cost to us came out at sixpence each. But then the war ended. The Taurus was not required and our first order, at 400 per cent profit, was the last.

As I mentioned earlier, we occupied a part of a disused cloth mill belonging to a very big and old established woollen cloth manufacturer named Marling & Evans. This mill stood on the river Frome, which provided the power to drive the machinery through a water wheel. The floor space was about 65,000sq.ft in a four-storey main building and several smaller single-storey detached buildings. Just before the war the machinery had been sent to Germany as scrap iron for their war factories.

There were many other stone-built mills like Port Mills in the Stroud area, several on the Frome and, when the bombing of London began, lots of London manufacturers tried to buy one of these mills to retreat to in case of need.

One of these was a Mr George Hensher, who owned three furniture factories in the Hackney district of London. He bought Port Mills from Marling & Evans, and a party of carpenters, electricians, plumbers, painters and labourers came down and spent several weeks preparing the mill for the transfer from London. Henscher became our landlord and agreed to us remaining as tenants on the same terms. He was a very amiable man but did not understand country ways.

In front of my office and within the factory boundaries was a small garden in which stood a caretaker's cottage next to a fair-sized building which had been used as a kind of a village hall and provided a meeting place for the W.I., the Nursing Association and so on. An old worker of Marling & Evans and his wife lived in the cottage rent-free, and no rent was paid for the village room. I think the name of the old people was Berry; anyway, that's what I will call them.

Although Hensher was pleasant to me, he could be very high-handed. He offended several people, in particular Mrs Berry, whom he treated as a caretaker, which she wasn't. She complained of it to me, while Hensher also lamented to me the attitude of the local people.

One day I had to speak to Mrs Berry about something and she began to sound off about Hensher and his wife, the latter of whom had apparently stepped on her flower bed to knock at the window and motioned her to come out. So the next time Hensher came to my office I said, 'You keep complaining about the attitude of local people to you. I wonder if you would be prepared to accept some advice on the matter without being offended.'

'All right', he said, 'Fire ahead.'

'Well', I said:

> The people down here aren't daft. They are not used to being pushed around and they don't like it. Ask them to do something and they'll do it. Tell them to do something and they won't. Mrs Berry in particular is incensed that your wife trod on her flowerbed and banged on the window to her to come out. She isn't paid by you, and neither she nor her husband will do anything for you. They can live in that house rent-free for life and you can't do anything about it. She also tells me you are going to use the village room for a canteen. Forget it. To you, the Berrys are nobodies. In the village they are respected citizens. She is a member of the W.I. and of the Nursing Association and secretary of the P.T.A. At the moment, because of her, your name in the village is mud. I suggest that from now on when you want to speak to her you go quietly through the gate and close it behind you. Then go down the path, knock reasonably on the door, and when she opens it raise your hat to her, saying 'good morning', speak to her politely, and when you leave raise your hat again and don't forget to close the door behind you.

'What!' he said, 'To that old woman? I'm damned if I do!'

'OK', I said, 'I can only tell you that if you don't, you'll be in the cart when you bring your business down here, for you'll get no work people. She has got more influence here than you have. Think it over.'

A few days later he told me that, although he had resented my advice at the time, he had decided to do as I said, and a few days after that, when I was talking to Mrs Berry, she said, 'That Mr Hensher isn't so bad when you get to know him.'

In fact, Hensher became quite popular. However, he never occupied the factory, for while I was talking to him one day, a man in a bowler hat and with a dispatch case and a rolled umbrella came up to us and asked, 'Which of you is the owner of this factory?'

On being told, he said, 'I'm sorry to have to inform you, but I am Commander — and I am commandeering the whole of the premises on behalf of the Admiralty. Here are my credentials and authority.'

Poor Hensher. He was absolutely stunned. Within days the factory was filled with lorry tyres, torpedo cases and other stores, and there they stayed until the end of the war. Other factories were also commandeered in the same way.

In 1944 I began to think of the future and sent out feelers to the Ministry of Agriculture to see if and when it might be possible to resume manufacture of Kinkades, as an order existed forbidding manufacture of such machines except by licence. I got a very dismissive answer. But the war was obviously moving towards a victorious end, war work was beginning to drop off and I was getting worried as to how we were going to keep employed the considerable work force we had built up.

I realised that if we were going to make a success of the manufacture of Kinkades and allied lines we should need more space and more capital, and I set about obtaining both.

Regarding space, the obvious course was to attempt to obtain possession of the rest of the factory, although it would take us a long time to occupy it completely. So I approached Hensher, knowing that he could never occupy it and would have to get rid of it. He agreed to let us have it at a bargain price of £5,000, to be paid off in instalments, acting as tenants paying rent while paying for the factory. This was very pleasing, and as the war drew to its close I signed the necessary agreement and took possession. But I still had the problem of getting the Admiralty to remove their stores and release the buildings.

During the war all sorts of restrictions had been placed on manufacturers, apart from the taking over of premises for stores and, realising that unless these restrictions were removed they were going to be severely handicapped in restarting their normal businesses, a group of businessmen in Stroud formed the Association of Stroud and District Manufacturers, which I joined. Its membership grew to the astonishing total of over 200 firms, engaged in manufacturing.

As soon as the war ended the association attacked government bureaucracy with considerable success, but the one big problem was how to get the various departments

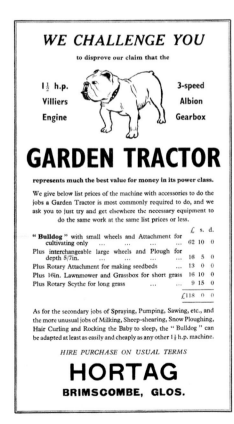

Hortag (Horticultural-Agricultural) was the name under which Arthur marketed mechanical equipment, including a spade of his own invention, during the late 1940s and 1950s. During the latter part of this period he, Vera and Nancy lived in Tibberton. He and Vera retired to Devon in the 1960s.

out of their premises. I attended a meeting one day at which all sorts of suggestions were made as to how this could be done, and it was finally decided to work through the local MP. I had become increasingly annoyed during the meeting and finally got up and said the suggestion to use the MP was useless, and they could count me out of any of their plans as I would act on my own and get my factory released and empty long before any of them. So I went home and wrote to Lord Beaverbrook, owner of the *Daily Express*, explaining the position. The next morning I had a phone call from the *Express* saying that a special reporter named, I think, Macaulay, was coming by train and I was to pick him up at Gloucester.

He proved to be about thirty and very switched on. I installed him in an office, told him the story and gave him all the files. I had his lunch and tea taken in to him and put him up in a guest house in Cainscross Road, where I stayed with him, working until about 2.30 a.m. He told me to pick him up in the morning and he would phone the story to the *Express*, and then I was to take him to catch a train at Gloucester for Birmingham at about noon. He completed the story, phoned it to London and I rushed him to Gloucester, racing alongside the incoming train down the Stroud Road. He rushed past the ticket inspector and got on the moving train, waved and shouted, 'Don't forget the *Daily Express*', and he was gone.

He had told me in the car that the article would appear in the *Express* the following morning, so early the next day I stopped in Stroud and with some trepidation approached W.H. Smith's, where I was somewhat embarrassed to find my own name staring at me from the top of a pile of *Daily Expresses*.

The article was entitled 'The 364 Letters of Mr Bullock', and the date was 26 October 1945. One of these papers accompanies this manuscript, and it tells its own story.[23]

All of this was dramatic enough, but the sequel was almost incredible. I proceeded to work with my bundle of papers, and showed Shepheard and Waddington, who had disapproved all along the way I was attacking the four ministries, warning me that my efforts were futile. By about 11 a.m. they had come up to my office for a cup of tea, and we were discussing the matter when my secretary came in to say there was an Army major outside who wanted to speak to me.

I asked her to bring him in, and after introducing himself he asked, much to my astonishment, where were the tyres which were to be moved. I enquired what tyres, and he explained that he had brought a convoy of lorries to move all the tyres and other stores from Port Mills. I could hardly believe it until he showed me through the window a convoy stretching from near our gates out of sight along the road to Stroud. I believe the number was over 200.

I asked him when he had received his orders and he said that it had been between eight and nine that morning, from the War Office, for immediate action.

I showed him the article in the paper, and he, too, was astonished.

All this took place within a few days of my leaving the meeting of my fellow manufacturers.

Afterword

by A.S. Bullock's daughter, Nancy Lewis

My father's memoirs cease on 26 October 1945 when he was forty-six years old. His business prospered for a few more years but the British horticultural industry, for which he made machinery, went through a difficult time due to foreign imports, and this adversely affected his business. Eventually he took early retirement and moved to Devon, where I was working as a welfare officer. There he fulfilled a useful voluntary role acting as secretary of several societies, including the Horticultural Association, and becoming a most entertaining and helpful grandparent to my four children, with my mother, to whom he was devoted. He loved life and remained fascinated by all aspects of it until his death on 5 June 1988 in his eighty-ninth year. His wife, Vera, died in 1994 aged ninety-four.

Spirings, Burlescombe, Devon – Arthur and Vera's home for most of their retirement. Their grandaughter Rachel did this felt-pen drawing aged fourteen, the same age as Arthur when he painted his first home sixty-eight years earlier (see chapter one). Vera is sweeping the porch, and the rickety gate that Arthur was about to replace is captured for posterity!

Vera and Arthur celebrating their Golden Wedding in 1978, photographed in the garden of Spirings with their four grandchildren, Rachel, Rosalind, Joanna and Edward Lewis.

Endnotes

1 Arthur began writing this memoir in the early 1970s.
2 Unfortunately, Arthur's family have been unable to locate the photograph, which reveals, by Arthur's scowl, that wearing a dress was not to his taste.
3 This was written in the mid-1970s, and Frank lived on for another quarter of a century after that.
4 WCs and washing facilities.
5 A.F. Barnes (ed.), *The Story of the 2/5th Gloucestershire Regiment, 1914–1918*, (Crypt House Press, Gloucester, 1930), page 88.
6 Ibid, page 100.
7 Ibid, page 117.
8 Ibid, page 133–8.
9 Ibid, page 136, bottom.
10 Ibid, page 39.
11 Ibid, page 140.
12 According to Philip Gibbs writing in *The New York Times*, 10 October 1918, the name was 'von Marwitz Kaserne'.
13 Arthur notes that the Glosters were billeted at Fransn.
14 Arthur noted here that he was writing this in 1973 while recovering from a heart attack.
15 This is the spelling from Arthur's sketchbook, while the manuscript has 'Chung Kamena Changwa'.
16 Floss outlived all her siblings and died in 1995 at the age of 105.
17 There are other stories told of Lucy's ability to tell character from handwriting, an aptitude also demonstrated by Arthur's daughter Nancy. Lucy's prediction about Arthur proved entirely correct, although, as his granddaughter Rachel writes, he may have been in part influenced by it, which would, of course, vindicate her reluctance to co-operate.
18 Arthur's granddaughter Rachel comments: 'It does not seem to have occurred to Arthur, who was generous in spirit, that the malevolent Carrington may have had a share in these two bouts of "bad luck".'
19 This name is difficult to discern from the manuscript.
20 Arthur here notes, perhaps with a touch of chagrin: 'I have just read the foregoing to my wife, who vigorously denies that she ever asked me to marry her.'
21 Arthur's granddaughter Rachel comments: 'In the 1920s it was assumed that married women would not continue with their careers. However, it is ironic that Arthur effectively stepped into his wife's shoes. It strikes me that my grandmother may well have resented it, but being a most reserved and discreet woman she kept any such thoughts to

herself. Evidently, this idea had not occurred to Arthur – even by 1981 when he wrote this!'

22 Arthur's grandaughter Rachel later worked for Lister-Petter (formerly R.A. Lister & Co.) and attended exhibitions at Dursley Town Hall and Dursley Heritage Centre to celebrate 140 years of the firm. One of the early items on display in both locations was Arthur's book, *Your Works and Ours*.

23 The front-page *Daily Express* article could not be located for inclusion in the book.

Index

Other titles published by The History Press

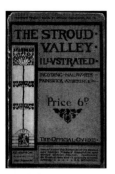

The Stroud Valley Illustrated

Stroud has witnessed many changes since the original version of this book was first published over 100 years ago. A fourth reprint, from 1911, was recently discovered in a local resident's collection, and contains many of the advertisements and photographs that were created at the time, giving the modern reader a glimpse into Stroud Valley life all those decades ago.

This valuable historical guide contains a cornucopia of photographs, advertisements and information relating to Stroud and its neighbouring villages and towns. It will certainly be a nostalgic read for those who have lived in the area for many years and members of local historical societies, and a fascinating insight for those visiting or new to the Five Valleys.

978 0 7524 4817 6

Les Pugh's Memories

LES PUGH

Les Pugh is well known in the Stroud area for his absorbing memories that have appeared over the years in the *Stroud News & Journal*. Recalling life from the early 1900s, these columns have now been collated into this fascinating book giving a glimpse of a life few now remember. Les has seen a great many changes during his lifetime and with his rare gift for recollecting intricate details from the past and the clarity of writing, the reader is will be absorbed by poignant memories of those far-off days.

978 0 7524 4791 1

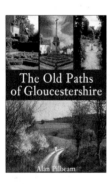

The Old Paths of Gloucestershire

ALAN PILBEAM

A walk around the old paths of Gloucestershire is, in many ways, a walk through the history of Gloucestershire itself. In this fascinating account, Alan Pilbeam takes us on a tour of the county's pathways and roads, demonstrating how the evolution of Gloucestershire society over time, from the pilgrims of the Middle Ages through the battle-scars of the Civil War and the industrial workers of the Victoria era, is reflected in changes in both the uses and nature of the county's footpaths.

Including 100 high-quality photographs, it is also an excellent introduction to walking in Gloucestershire and will prove invaluable to both visitors to the area and locals

978 0 7524 4540 3

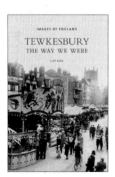

Tewkesbury
The Way We Were
CLIFF BURD

The county town of Tewkesbury stands on a flood plain, surrounded by water on all sides, with two major rivers and several smaller brooks which have always flooded. Flooding in the nineteenth century through to 2007 and Tewkesbury's most severe flood in living memory, will bring back graphic memories of how the people of the town worked together to overcome these difficult times. The town has seen little in the way of major industry with the majority of people working in two or three jobs at a time to make ends meet. This volume endeavours to show how leisure activities have changed over the past century with many of the images showing sporting groups, fairs and festive activities.

978 0 7524 4692 9

Visit our website where you will discover our whole range of books covering all aspects of history

www.thehistorypress.co.uk